Canada A Portrait

$\mathcal{T}$HE OFFICIAL HANDBOOK OF PRESENT CONDITIONS AND RECENT PROGRESS • 55TH EDITION
PUBLISHED UNDER THE AUTHORITY OF THE MINISTER OF INDUSTRY

© Minister of Industry, 1995

Available in Canada through:

Authorized Bookstore Agents
and other bookstores

or by mail from:

Statistics Canada
Marketing Division
Sales and Service
120 Parkdale Avenue
Ottawa, Ontario
K1A 0T6
Telephone (613) 951-7277
Toll Free Order Line 1-800-267-6677 (Canada and U.S.A.)
Facsimile Number (613) 951-1584
Internet: order@statcan.ca

Friesens
Altona, Manitoba

The National Library of Canada has catalogued this publication as follows:

Main entry under title:

Canada: A Portrait

55th ed.
Biennial
"The official handbook of present conditions and recent progress."
Issued also in French under title: Un portrait du Canada,
Continues: Canada handbook, the...handbook of present
conditions and recent progress.
ISBN 0-660-15570-2

1. Canada – Economic conditions - Periodicals.
2. Canada – Social conditions - Periodicals.
3. Canada – Politics and government - Periodicals.
4. Canada – Description and travel - Periodicals.
5. Canada – Handbooks, manuals, etc. I. Statistics Canada.
Communications Division.

La présente publication est également disponible en français.

Printed in Canada

FOREWORD At Statistics Canada, we are committed to presenting the information we collect – from all Canadians – in a way that everyone can understand and use.

Relying on the talent and energy of Canadians from all walks of life and drawing on a rich legacy of Canadian art, photography and literature, *Canada: A Portrait* continues to break new ground in the presentation of statistics. I am especially honoured to signal the contributions of six very accomplished Canadians who brought their own unique visions of Canada to our "portrait." Many thanks to Myriam Bédard, Graham Greene, Evelyn Hart, Gerhard Herzberg, Julie Payette, and Joe Schlesinger.

The *Portrait* first appeared in 1927 on the occasion of the 60th anniversary of Canada's founding. With this 55th edition, it endures as an important record of the social, economic and artistic life of Canada. I recommend it to all our readers with great pride.

Ivan P. Fellegi

Chief Statistician of Canada

ACKNOWLEDGEMENTS *Canada: A Portrait* is one of those rare projects which combines both the creative and the analytic. In this process, it has been strengthened by the vision and commitment of all who worked on it. Together with Wayne Smith, Director of Communications, and Krista Campbell, Production Manager, I am honoured to signal the contributions of the *Portrait* team.

Two editorial teams worked side by side. Senior French Editor Nathalie Turcotte, with Nadine Lemoine, brought a fresh perspective to the French edition, while David Gonczol, Liz Hart, Jocelyn Harvey, Sarah Hubbard, Tom Vradenburg and Daniel Woolford met the challenge of writing technical prose with lyric and literary vigor. Yves Thériault of Public Works and Government Services and Jeannot Trudel provided solid translations and Martin Blais, editorial consultation. Many thanks to all.

Special mention must also go to David Gonczol for assiduous and excellent research work, Neil Walsh for careful proofreading and to Maxine Davidson, Production Assistant, for her humour and grace under pressure.

Much appreciation is extended to Jim Reil, editorial consultant, and to Tanis Browning-Shelp and Denis Bernard who have gone on to new challenges from their inspired work with the *Portrait* team.

Canada: A Portrait is reviewed by referees within Statistics Canada. For their invaluable insights and guidance we wish to thank

Mary Cromie, Philip Cross, Tim Davis, Jean Dumas, Barry Haydon, Iain McKellar, Craig McKie, Roger Purdue, Paul Reed and Philip Smith. As well, many took the time to offer assistance with particular areas, including Ken Bennett, Adele Furrie, Gerry Gravel, Paul McPhie, Douglas Palmer, Garnett Picot, Henry Puderer, Rob Riordan and Michael Wolfson.

A special management group exists at Statistics Canada to advise and guide the *Portrait* team. Many thanks to its members: Denis Desjardins, Louis Boucher, Bob Freeman, Martin Podehl, David Roy and Wayne Smith.

Special thanks to John MacCraken, Manager of Graphic Design, Renée Saumure and Michael McAuliffe, design analysts, and Danielle Baum, Manager of Production Integration, for their careful attention to the details. For compelling speed, we wish to acknowledge the desktop publishing team, headed by Johanne Beauseigle and consisting of Louise Demers, Diane Joanisse and Francine Simoneau.

Our appreciation is also extended to Jacques Téssier, Printing Consultant, and general shepherd of the project through the printing world, as well as Barbara Elliott and Carol Misener in printing liaison.

For an innovative marketing strategy, many thanks to Kathryn Bonner, Marketing Co-ordinator, and her team consisting of Mary Rigby and Kate James. We would also like to extend our sincere appreciation to the staff of Statistics Canada's library.

They have offered us outstanding support and insightful guidance in our research for this publication.

We wish to especially honour the work of Neville Smith and Aviva Furman who have renewed the design of the *Portrait*, bringing both a sense of beauty and balance to the presentation of the information. Also, a special thanks to Eric Walker for a studied and careful approach to the research of the photographs.

Finally, I wish to acknowledge Wayne Smith, for inspiring leadership and guidance through the project and Krista Campbell, for her enthusiasm and gracious competence. I have been privileged to work with these people.

Jonina Wood

Editor-in-Chief, *Canada: A Portrait*

OUR THANKS TO YOU...the millions of Canadians who take the time to answer our questions. Your support makes it possible to produce books such as this and to offer to you information about the people, land, economy and culture which surrounds you.

From all of us at Statistics Canada, our sincere thanks.

TABLE OF CONTENTS

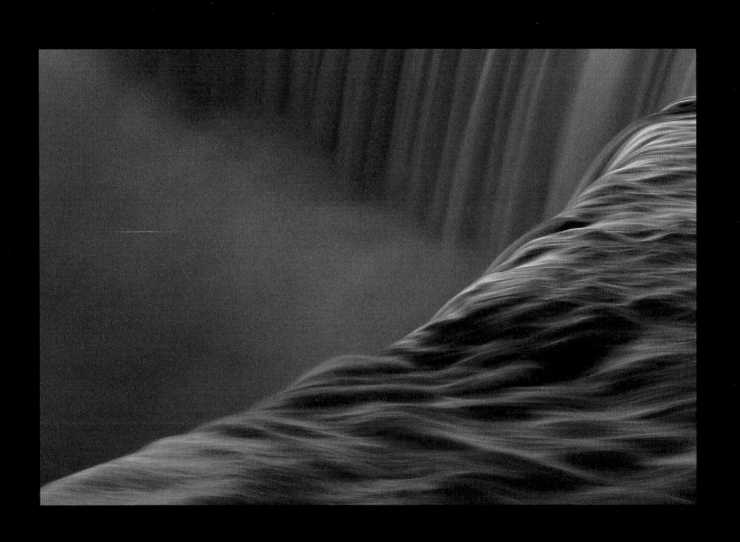

*W*hen I was a young person, I trained as a cadet with the Canadian army, making my way to the Arctic Circle and to the Rockies, and sleeping outside as I went. I began a great love affair with this country and its wildness.

Now when I train, I may go 30 kilometres deep into the bush, finding strength in the sheer wildness around me. It can get so wild that I come face to face with grizzlies and brown bears. But it is also very freeing, connecting me to a sense of space and speed. Canada, for me, is this wildness; it is as vital to my sport as the air I breathe.

Myriam Bédard, born in Neufchâtel, Quebec. First Canadian woman to win 2 gold medals at the same Winter Olympic Games.

The Land

Of Canada, Margaret Atwood has written: "In a country with such a high ratio of trees, lakes and rocks to people, images from Nature are almost everywhere." Whimsical but true. In Canada, some 70% of the land is wilderness – land with no sign of human settlement.

As Canadians, we celebrate this: our novels, poems, songs, our national anthem, our conversation, our newspapers are all rich with images of the land.

The land challenges us to describe it, and we take up the challenge. "No European except for a Russian can ever take in the size of Canada except by travelling by train," writes author Mavis Gallant. "A long plane journey gives some idea, particularly at night when the lights of cities are like rafts in what seems to be the emptiest and darkest of seas."

Canada's size makes it the second largest country in the world, topped only by the Russian Federation. We have 7% of the world's land mass, and 9% of its fresh water supply. Of a total area of nearly ten million square kilometres, over nine million are land, and 755,000 fresh water. The three oceans that couch our shores – the Atlantic, the Pacific and the Arctic – provide us with the world's longest coastline at 244,000 kilometres.

Given Canada's image as "the great white North," it may come as a surprise to find that our southernmost land is an island that shares a latitude with Northern California to the west and Rome to the east. Appropriately named Middle Island, it sits in the middle of the Lake Erie shipping channel just north of the 41st parallel. The most southerly occupied land is nearby Pelee Island near Point Pelee, Ontario, a national park and mecca for bird-watchers.

The True North? It took more than a century of debate to pinpoint the precise location of Canada's northern extremity. Finally, in 1987, the Department of National Defence determined that it was a small point extending from Cape Columbia on Ellesmere Island at a latitude of 83°06′41.35″ N. From this point to our southernmost point, Canada stretches 4,634 kilometres.

East to west, the width of the country is such that Newfoundlanders are already at lunch when British Columbians are having breakfast. Canada spans six time zones: there's a four-and-a-half hour difference between Pacific Time and Newfoundland Time. Canada's most easterly land (and that of North America too) is Cape Spear near St. John's, Newfoundland. The most westerly is the Yukon-Alaska boundary, 5,514 kilometres away.

Tying this country together is the world's longest national highway. The Trans-Canada Highway runs from St. John's, Newfoundland on the Atlantic Ocean to Victoria, British Columbia on the Pacific, an asphalt ribbon nearly 8,000 kilometres long.

STARTING POINT "Canada begins right here," proclaims the sign at St. John's City Hall, Mile 0/ Kilometre 0 of the Trans-Canada Highway. Author Farley Mowat has described Newfoundland as "a mighty granite stopper over the bellmouth of the Gulf of St. Lawrence."

In fact, the province is made up of the island of Newfoundland, and Labrador, part of the mainland. The scenery is best described as rocky; Labrador is covered by thick forests to the south and barren mountain peaks to the north. According to Canada's climate severity index, the residents of St. John's experience the most severe weather in Canada: their days are the foggiest, snowiest, wettest, windiest and cloudiest.

In 1994, Newfoundland was one of only two regions (the other being Yukon Territory) to lose population. That year, Newfoundlanders numbered 582,000, down 2,000 from the previous year. With a total area of 406,000 square kilometres, Newfoundland has the lowest provincial population density (1.6 people per square kilometre).

In terms of natural resources, for generations Newfoundlanders have depended on their fishery. Now, with this industry in decline, Newfoundlanders are having to find other means of livelihood and, in some cases, are moving elsewhere. However, Newfoundland is Canada's leading source of iron ore; in 1992, the province produced almost 18 million tonnes.

THE ISLAND "Fair Island of the Sea" is how Lucy Maud Montgomery, creator of Anne of Green Gables, described her home province. And with its red soil and white, sandy beaches, Prince Edward Island has a distinctive beauty. Much of it is farmland, with potato and mixed grain fields covering 45% of the island.

At 5,660 square kilometres, "the Island" is Canada's smallest province, but it actually has the country's highest provincial population density: about 23 people for every square kilometre, although the total population is under 135,000. The province is also the least urbanized, with just 40% of Islanders living in towns or cities.

The natural beauty of the Maritime provinces – Prince Edward Island, Nova Scotia and New Brunswick – makes them a popular summer vacation destination, but winter brings widely seesawing temperatures and heavy storms.

NOVA SCOTIA With much of its land edged by the rugged North Atlantic, Nova Scotia is a province of the ocean. Famous for the *Bluenose* schooner, Canada's fishing and sailing champion of the 1920s, its inhabitants are often affectionately called "Bluenosers," even to this day.

The province is also famous for its musical talent: the Barra MacNeils, Rita MacNeil, Ashley MacIsaac, the Rankin Family and many more have brought acclaim to Nova Scotia.

Schooners and crooners aside, Nova Scotia has traditionally relied on fishing, but this is now an industry in trouble. On the other hand, Nova Scotia has a larger and more diverse manufacturing sector than the other two Maritime provinces. The province's principal mineral is coal, the production of which in 1992 was worth $265 million.

Most of the population of 937,000 live somewhere within 10 kilometres of salt water, but then no part of Nova Scotia is more than 50 kilometres from the sea. The province covers 55,000 square kilometres and includes Cape Breton Island, now joined to the mainland by a permanent causeway.

PICTURE PROVINCE   New Brunswick has been called the picture province with the lush green of farmlands and forests and the cool blue of the St. John River. The province is small, only 73,440 square kilometres, and much remains treed, approximately 90%. Forestry dominates New Brunswick's economy. The pulp and paper and forestry and wood products industries account for 6% of all jobs and about 40% of provincial exports.

The St. John River, as much as the forests, has influenced the development of the province. Flowing southerly, through the middle of the province, it was a major transportation route for traders, loggers and shippers during the late 18th and 19th centuries. It remains the lifeblood of the farmland that stretches along much of its banks. Perfect for some crops, this land produced about 16% of Canada's potatoes in 1994, one of New Brunswick's major crops. In the south, the pasture land provides suitable grazing land for dairy and beef cattle. The river is also a source of power; about 90% of the province's hydro-electric energy is fuelled by the St. John River.

New Brunswick retains much of the spirit and ways of its settlers. As Canada's only officially bilingual province, it achieves a balance between the largely Loyalist settlers of the south and the Acadian settlers of the north. Today, the province has a Francophone minority of 34%, which has remained fairly stable over the past 20 years.

LA BELLE PROVINCE   It's large and it's beautiful: about 80% of "la belle province" is covered by the Canadian Shield, a mosaic of forests, rocky outcrops, lakes and rivers. The fertile lowlands of the St. Lawrence River counterbalance this wildness with their robust dairy and livestock industries.

Quebec is Canada's largest province, covering 1.5 million square kilometres. Of that area, 184,000 square kilometres are water: Quebec has a quarter of Canada's fresh water.

In 1994, the population of Quebec was 7.3 million, about 5.2 people for every square kilometre. Most Quebecers (78%) live in the province's towns and cities.

About half of all Canadians live in the corridor between Quebec and Windsor, Ontario. One of the area's natural advantages is its closeness to the St. Lawrence River and the Great Lakes. The St. Lawrence Seaway, opened in 1959, links the five Great Lakes and the St. Lawrence River with the Atlantic Ocean, providing an economical means of shipping bulk commodities such as grain, iron ore and coal.

Quebecers produce about one-quarter of Canadian manufactured goods – mostly paper, primary metals and processed foods. The province is one of the world's leading producers of asbestos. It produces Canada's second largest quantity of gold after Ontario, and of iron ore after Newfoundland, and is also a major producer of copper.

Montreal, the largest urban centre in this province, may be the snow removal capital of the world. Of all major cities, it clears the most snow from its streets, an average of 42 million tonnes a year. This reality moved Montreal poet Émile Nelligan to write: "Oh! How the snow snowed!"

ONTARIO Pianist Glenn Gould found Ontario countryside "absolutely haunting in its emptiness and bleakness and starkly magnificent beauty." But with all this largely true, Ontario is still where over one-third of us live: close to 11 million in 1994.

As in Quebec, the Canadian Shield dominates the province but the climate and soil of the Great Lakes lowlands make Ontario the provincial leader in agricultural production at $5 billion in 1991 (a quarter of Canada's total). At the same time, the province is Canada's industrial heartland, accounting for about half the country's manufacturing. The manufacture of transportation equipment is its largest single industry. Ontario also leads Canada in the production of gold and nickel.

Ontario is home to Canada's largest metropolitan area, Toronto, with 4.3 million inhabitants in 1994. It shares the National Capital Region with Quebec: Ottawa-Hull, with just over one million inhabitants, is Canada's fourth largest metropolitan area after Montreal and Vancouver.

PRAIRIE POOL "Moving from east to west the land/rises in successive giant steps/like prairie billiard tables," wrote poet Al Purdy of this part of Canada. Table-top flat for the most part, the Prairies encompass Manitoba, Saskatchewan and Alberta, and are covered by the deep fertile clay soils left by glacial lakes. Hot summers and cold winters are the norm here, with relatively light precipitation in all seasons. The area is largely built on agriculture, with wheat and other grain crops being the most important.

Manitoba Cool "If I am asked what my image of Manitoba is," said novelist Gabrielle Roy, "the one that comes to mind spontaneously is that of the giant plain, open, immense, yet tender and full of dreams." Manitoba is Canada's geographic heartland. Its southern plain is the lowest of the three step-like formations of the Prairie region, and is covered by deep, fertile soil. Winnipeg, the capital of Manitoba, has the distinction of being the coldest major city in Canada, with a January mean temperature of -18°C.

About 1.1 million people live in Manitoba, of whom 72% are urban dwellers. Apart from agriculture, the province's economy is based on manufacturing, mineral production (Manitoba is second to Ontario in production of nickel), and a small commercial freshwater fishery.

Saskatchewan "And Saskatchewan and Saskatchewan and Saskatchewan: said the train."

Author Malcolm Lowry's words evoke the rhythm of the train trekking across the great plains of this province. One of Canada's most palpable symbols has been its rail system. In fact, the steel rails of the transcontinental railways built in the late 19th and early 20th centuries welded the nation together and fuelled its industrialization. They also brought the flood of agricultural immigrants to the Prairies.

More land area is given over to farms in Saskatchewan than in any other province. Known as the "bread basket of the nation," the province has a total land area of 570,700 square kilometres, of which farming takes up 47%. Despite this, the province's population of just over one million lives mostly in cities (63%).

While the leading industry is agriculture, Saskatchewan is also a major world producer of potash. In 1992, it was the Canadian leader in the production of uranium (eight million kilograms), and was second to Alberta in the value of petroleum produced ($1.4 billion).

And Alberta "I want to scribble all over that enormous sky!" novelist Marian Engel once exclaimed. While Alberta claims the famous Rocky Mountains as its western border, most of the province lies in the plains. Alberta's 2.7 million residents experience a highly variable winter climate: the Chinook arch, a strong, warm southwestern wind sweeping over the Rockies from the Pacific Ocean, can raise the temperature 15°C in an hour.

Alberta is oil country. It accounts for about half the value of mineral production in Canada ($16.4 billion). Almost all of this comes from petroleum, and natural gas and its by-products. Grain and livestock production are also important to the provincial economy.

BRITISH COLUMBIA Humorist Eric Nicol has called it "a large body of land entirely surrounded by envy." Indeed, the province's natural beauty, together with its mild climate, makes it increasingly a desirable place to live.

Over the past two decades, the trend has in fact been westward. British Columbia has Canada's fastest growing population: in 1994, there were 3.7 million British Columbians, an increase of 2.6% over the previous year – a growth rate more than double the national average. Both immigrants and other Canadians contribute to British Columbia's population growth.

British Columbia's economy thrives on its natural resources, the forest industry being the most important. In 1991, the province led Canada in the value of forest products ($3.8 billion). In 1992, it was also number one in the value of coal produced ($706 million) and copper ($908 million). Livestock, specialty crops and fruit are the major agricultural products. The extensive fishery – Canada's largest – is based on salmon and herring.

YUKON "If the North has a soul," Pierre Berton has mused, "it is here in this empty land which, harsh though it is, has a beauty that no man who has not lived there a lifetime can really understand." This triangle of plateaus and mountains covers 483,000 square kilometres. Mount Logan, at 5,959 metres the highest point in Canada, is located in the St. Elias Mountains in the southwest. Yukon has the greatest average annual temperature range in North America, at 40°C. As with the Northwest Territories, the population is sparse: with some 30,000 people, there are only 0.1 people for each square kilometre. Mining is the chief economic activity.

NORTHWEST TERRITORIES This vast area of 3.4 million square kilometres – one-third of Canada – features extremes in topography, flora and fauna, and climate. Most of the area is plains, but in the extreme north are mountainous highlands. There are many fur-bearing animals and species of fish, and brilliantly blooming plant life during the brief, cool summers. The climate is harsh with long, cold winters, although surprisingly little snow. This is the land of the midnight sun and the polar night, where the sun remains below the horizon for several weeks at midwinter.

Because of the climate and poorly developed soils, this is the most sparsely populated region of the country with just 64,000 inhabitants. Population density is a mere 0.02 people per square kilometre. The economy is dominated by the mining industry; fur and fisheries are exploited commercially on a small scale.

NATURAL RESOURCES Canada has an abundant supply of natural resources – land, water, minerals and wildlife – on which our economy still depends to a large extent.

"Free 160 acre Western Canada farm lands," exclaimed

Immigration Branch advertising at the turn of the century, and many came to Canada with dreams of farmland as far as the eye could see, although forest was more often the reality. In 1991, we had 460,000 square kilometres of cropland. Of course, that's only 5% of our land area. Another 3.6% is permanent pasture.

Forest – 4.5 million square kilometres of it – still covers more of this land than anything else and is the basis for an important industry in Canada. In 1991, the 162 million cubic metres of wood produced accounted for $7.7 billion in revenues.

Canada's water supply would appear almost inexhaustible: we use just 1.5% of the renewable supply. Canadians are the world's second largest users of water, next to our neighbours to the south. Each one of us typically uses 340 litres a day – about two-and-a-half bathtubs full.

Canada holds 6% of the world's 15 most important minerals. Metallic minerals (such as gold, copper and zinc) and petroleum are the most valuable. And we produce half as much energy again as we use, making Canada a net energy exporter.

Canada has a wealth of wildlife. If you're an entomologist, Canada could be the country for you: we have almost 34,000 known species of insects, and another 33,000 are believed to exist! At the other end of the scale, Canada is home to just 83 known species of amphibians and reptiles.

A CALL TO ACTION To encourage Canadians to "tree Canada," the National Community Tree Foundation is distributing tiny tree-growing kits containing 8 to 10 tree seeds, a water-resistant growing box about the size of a baby food jar, and growing materials. The seedlings can eventually be transferred outdoors where they may live for up to 80 years. One large tree can discharge 450 litres of water into the air in one day, lowering the temperature around it in summer by 5 to 9 degrees, and reducing energy consumption by air conditioners; and it can provide a day's oxygen for up to four people.

WASTE NOT, WANT NOT Agropur, an agri-food co-operative owned by some 4,500 Quebec milk producers, has taken care of its pollution problem and, in the process, is saving at least $150,000 a year.

In 1993, Agropur, which makes milk, cheese and yogurt, installed a wastewater treatment system that produces methane. The gas in turn produces enough energy to operate the plant's machinery. As well as conserving land, saving energy and preventing the discharge of wastewater into the Nicolet River, a tributary of the St. Lawrence, the process yields a sludge that can be used as agricultural fertilizer.

HEAD COUNT Canada, with its abundance of area and its richness of resources, was bound to attract people. Nevertheless, we're relatively poor in population.

On July 1, 1994, it was estimated that Canadians numbered 29.2 million, up 1.1 million from July 1991. This is a mere fiftieth of the population of China, however, in a comparable land area.

Canada's population density is just 3.2 people per square kilometre as against China's 124.

While our numbers are increasing, our rate of growth is slowing down. As of July 1994, Canada's population growth had slowed to 1.1% per year from an average 1.2% a year between 1981 and 1991.

But Canada is still growing faster than any other Western industrialized nation. The typical growth rate in developed countries is less than 1% per year; in developing countries, it's around 2%.

Reflecting a general trend in population distribution, in 1994 most immigrants chose to live in Ontario. However, that province's share of the total number of immigrants dropped from 55% in 1993 to 51% in 1994, while British Columbia's share increased from 15% to 21%.

Canadians are largely urban dwellers. In 1991, three-quarters of us lived in towns and cities, and were within a two-hour drive of the United States.

ENVIRONMENT SCOPE Canadian cities are associated with fresh air and blue sky in sharp contrast to the smog of big international cities. But our city air can also be laden with all the chemicals of modern life.

To judge the strength of this urban cocktail, we have devised the Air Quality Index (AQI). The AQI tells us whether it's safe to breathe on a given day. In fact, Canada's urban air quality has improved over the past decade. According to the AQI, even the residents of an industrial area such as Hamilton breathe good air about 60% of the time, and poor air only 6% of the time. In comparison, Haligonians and those in Regina breathe good air 99.7% of the time and never breathe what the AQI terms poor quality air.

But, if Canada's air is improving, global atmospheric issues are still a concern. The erosion of the ozone layer is one such issue. This natural sunscreen has been steadily eroding, primarily because of chemicals such as chlorofluorocarbons (CFCs). Canada has been a leader in eliminating CFC production, and has agreed to phase it out altogether by 1997.

Another issue is global warming. "Greenhouse" gases help keep the Earth at the right temperature, but too much of them could cause it to overheat. Carbon dioxide, from deforestation and the burning of coal, oil and natural gas, is a major contributor. Canadians may feel we have energy to burn, but our affluent lifestyle puts us among the world's highest carbon dioxide producers. Canada is aiming to stabilize greenhouse gas emissions at 1990 levels by 2000.

FOREST NATION Canada has been called a "forest nation." Most of subarctic Canada is covered to some degree by forest. Forest and woodland occupy 39% of Canada's land area. To Canadians, forests mean much more than the value of their timber. Besides economic returns and employment, forests provide recreational space and habitat for wildlife, conserve water and soil, and help to control the climate and purify the air.

Forests are crucial to the Canadian economy. In 1991, Canada was the world's largest exporter of forest products. In 1992, the forest industries were responsible for 3% of the Gross Domestic Product and 15% of all exports. In 1991, Canadians harvested timber from 859 million hectares, most of it by clear-cutting. British Columbia foresters harvested more than twice the volume of wood harvested in any other province, although Quebecers and Ontarians harvested from larger areas.

Inevitably, the harvesting of timber results in loss of, or change in, forest cover. It also provides access to previously wild areas by roads constructed for forestry operations.

Canada's forest area increased marginally between 1965 and 1989. While much of the forest is regenerated naturally, the

BIG YELLOW TAXI

They took all the trees
And put them in a tree museum
And they charged all the people
A dollar and a half just to see 'em.
Don't it always seem to go
That you don't know what you've got
Till it's gone
They paved paradise
And put up a parking lot.

Hey farmer farmer
Put away that D.D.T. now
Give me spots on my apples
But leave me the birds and the bees
Please!
Don't it always seem to go
That you don't know what you've got
Till it's gone
They paved paradise
And put up a parking lot.

Joni Mitchell

planting of new trees and other silviculture activities are helping the regeneration and growth. At the United Nations (UN) Conference on Environment and Development in 1992 (also known as the Earth Summit), Canada endorsed the statement of principles on the management, conservation and sustainable development of forests.

Wetlands have been described as the kidneys of the environment: they filter water and reduce pollution. They also provide habitat for birds, fish and shellfish. Canada has one-quarter of the world's wetlands. Almost all Canada's urban wetlands have been converted to other uses, as well as most southern Ontario and St. Lawrence Valley swamps.

Other hard-hit areas are the Prairie sloughs (critical habitat to more than 50% of North America's waterfowl), and the Pacific and Atlantic marshes. The loss of wetlands is mostly due to agricultural expansion.

Agriculture has had the most widespread physical impact on the environment while accounting for just 7% of total land use. The Prairies, for example, have been altered perhaps more than any other area in Canada. About 87% of the natural grassland of southern Manitoba, Saskatchewan and Alberta has been turned into cropland, rangelands and pasture.

More people and more economic development have made it essential to conserve natural space for wildlife. Canada's objective is to protect 12% of its land area for this purpose. In 1993, we were close to our goal with 788,000 square kilometres (8.5%) of protected land. Protecting freshwater and marine areas is becoming more important. Non-government organizations are getting into the act: in 1993, Ducks Unlimited Canada headed the list with 7,900 wetland sites.

WELLSPRING Canada is wealthy in water. Water surrounds us, plaiting its way across the landscape as lakes, rivers and streams, and covering 8% of Canada's total area. Canadian lakes inform the Canadian way of life as we summer by them, cool off in them and, often, dump our wastes in them. They also contribute to the economy: in 1990, our abundant fresh water provided commercial fisheries with over $66 million worth of fish.

People have historically used bodies of water as convenient waste disposal systems, and Canadians are no exception. We have introduced thousands of pollutants into our water supply, including toxic dioxins and furans that accumulate in fish and other organisms downstream from pulp and paper mills using chlorine bleaching.

But there has been some progress. Regulations imposed in the 1970s have already had a beneficial effect on the Great Lakes. In 1994, regulations that imposed new limits on dioxins and furans in liquid industrial wastes from the pulp and paper industry came into force.

Industrial waste discharges with their highly toxic pollutants are more difficult to treat than regular municipal wastewater. Treatment levels vary considerably across the country. Overall, in 1991, 75% of Canadians were served by municipal sewage systems. Of these, 84% had some level of treatment applied to their wastewater, up from 72% in 1983.

SEA TO SEA "For Newfoundlanders living by and upon it," writes Farley Mowat, "the sea is the ultimate reality." For tens of thousands in Atlantic Canada and Quebec, this reality has become a great hardship. In 1992, due to a decline in fishstocks, the federal government declared a two-year moratorium on fishing for northern cod, the most important stock on the Atlantic coast. By the end of 1993, it had closed all but one Atlantic fishery for the 1994 season.

The reason for the decline is unclear. Some point to overfishing by national and foreign fisheries, others blame abusive fishing practices (such as dumping and discarding), predation by seals, or adverse environmental conditions.

The Pacific coast fisheries, too, appear to be dealing with a similar problem as they face the mystery of the missing salmon. In 1994, the number of salmon returning to the Fraser River spawning grounds was lower than anticipated. The salmon fishery is the most valuable on the Pacific coast. An independent review board is looking for answers.

To help ensure a sustainable supply of fish and seafood, Canadians are developing an aquaculture industry. Aquaculture is the business of raising fish and seafood in a managed environment. Currently, Canadian aquaculturalists are raising salmon, trout, oysters, scallops and mussels. In 1994, the industry generated over $290 million in revenue and employed more than 5,200 people.

The presence of toxic chemicals in some parts of the Great Lakes and St. Lawrence River watershed has seriously contaminated the food chain, including many fish. According to the St. Lawrence National Institute of Ecotoxicology, beluga whale carcasses on shore should be considered toxic waste. Providing a sanctuary for these animals is one of the reasons for the creation of the Saguenay Marine Park where the St. Lawrence and Saguenay rivers meet. The federal government is developing marine parks to make people aware of our natural marine heritage and to provide areas for marine research.

AT RISK In Canada, the list of species at risk is alarmingly long: 216 species as of 1993. For example, stocks of the Ungava Bay population of beluga whales have been reduced by hunting and ship traffic to the point where they are in immediate danger of extinction. The peregrine falcon barely exists in Canada, probably because toxic contaminants have led to reproductive failure. The aurora trout no longer exists in the wild and is being maintained only by captive breeding. Managing hunting and fishing, and establishing wildlife reserves have been the primary response to this situation. And there are success stories. The once-threatened white pelican has been removed from the list of species at risk, and the wood bison is now considered threatened rather than endangered. The peregrine falcon population also appears to be recovering.

In 1992, Canada ratified the UN Convention on Biological Diversity (biodiversity), and is now developing a Canadian biodiversity strategy. It sets out a vision for Canada as a society that values all life, that takes no more from nature than nature can replenish, and that leaves to future generations a world rich in biodiversity.

ONE WITH THE EARTH

Canadian architect Douglas Cardinal has written "We and the earth are one — what we do to the land we do to one another." Increasingly, Canadians are mindful of the spirit of this message, although much remains to be done.

Garbage Canadian households generate some 10 million tonnes of solid waste a year, produce 64,000 tonnes of hazardous waste, and consume 23% of Canada's energy. If you break the numbers down, however, it is easier to see that one person *can* make a difference.

In 1990, the typical Canadian home disposed of 2.5 kilograms of garbage a day. By far the two highest components of residential waste, according to a 1989 Ontario study, were paper, including newsprint, and food and yard waste.

Many of us can and do recycle much of what we used to consider garbage. In 1991, about half of all Canadian households had access to either curbside recycling or recycling depots for paper, glass and metal cans. Of those with access to recycling, 86% used the service. And some of us (17%) are composting or taking advantage of municipal yard waste pick-up.

Energy Canadians are among the highest energy consumers in the world. But we are becoming more energy-conscious. In 1993, 45% reported lowering our thermostats at night. Next to heating our homes, we used the most energy on heating water. However, 39% of homes had low-flow showerheads, about a third of us usually washed our laundry in cold water, and three-quarters of us rinsed it in cold water.

Wheels Canadians are wild about wheels — in 1992, we owned or leased 13 million private vehicles.

Automobiles are a significant contributor to carbon monoxide levels. Nonetheless, between 1987 and 1991, levels of carbon monoxide averaged well below acceptable limits in major Canadian cities.

Waste Not   One of Canada's fastest-growing industries is the environmental industry. Canadians have improved incinerator technologies, and invented new clean-up technologies and methods of using and recycling waste; we've pioneered the use of computers in natural resource management as well as innovative uses of remote sensing.

In 1994, some 4,500 environmental firms employed approximately 150,000 people. Annual sales totalled $11 billion, with $1 billion coming from the export of goods and services. The Global Opportunities for Business and the Environment (GLOBE) trade fair held every other year in Vancouver is the largest exposition of environmental goods and services in the world.

Planet Summit   In 1992, the Earth Summit set out a plan of action on the environment and development issues known as Agenda 21. Following the Summit, Canadians established the *Projet de société*, a partnership of more than 80 sectors of Canadian society managed by the National Round Table on the Environment and the Economy. The *Projet de société,* Canada's only national process working to create a sustainable development strategy, has invited all Canadians to a new relationship with the land.

ACA NADA   The origin and meaning of the name Canada has been a matter of surmise since the arrival of the first explorer. Jacques Cartier, reporting on his 1535-36 voyage, noted that *kanata* was an Iroquois word meaning town, or cluster of dwellings. Other reports have it that early Spanish or Portuguese explorers, disappointed in not finding gold or other riches, derided the country as *aca nada* or *cà nada* (here nothing). Yet others have ascribed the word to Latin or Sanskrit. The weight of opinion to date, however, favours the Aboriginal origin noted in Cartier's report. Whatever the source, the *Constitution Act, 1867,* Canada's original constitution, announced that the name of the new dominion would be...Canada.

REMEMBER "DOMINION?" There was Dominion Day, the Dominion Fire Commissioner and, of course, the Dominion of Canada. But now, we're Canada. Single-word names are fashionable today but in 1866, when representatives of the soon-to-be-formed nation assembled in London, a more grand and inspirational moniker was needed. Sir Samuel Leonard Tilley proposed the addition of the words "the Dominion of" to our name, inspired by his devotional readings and his desire to give us a name in keeping with our size and potential.

🍁

In 1935, I came to Canada, a refugee from Germany and the Nazis. I travelled by train across the Prairies on my way to

Saskatoon. As we passed through small railway stations, I would see perhaps two or three houses, a grain elevator. Where

were the people? I wondered.

But when I arrived in Saskatoon, I found them. These people were curious, kind and friendly, and they had the time to listen to

me, and my story. I settled into work at the University of Saskatchewan and found colleagues of considerable repute.

Canada is really the country that saved me. I have a sort of a hunch that Canada *is* my country.

The Honourable Gerhard Herzberg. Distinguished Research Scientist emeritus, National Research Council, Nobel laureate.

ON BEING CANADIAN In 1973, Pierre Berton, author, historian and favourite Canadian uncle, wrote lyrically that "...a Canadian is somebody who knows how to make love in a canoe."

Comforting, Berton's definition of being Canadian offered a certain simplicity, charm, even romance. But in fact, the struggle for a definition has grown more complicated.

The Canada of the 1990s looks different. The cities are bigger, Canadians are aging, and changing immigration patterns have introduced new faces and new voices to this land. Our family life has altered...with new arrangements, new definitions.

While most Canadians consider this country the best place on the planet, we are less certain about how to protect what we care about. We are still trying, for example, to agree to a set of definitive "Canadian" values. As we try to comprehend this latest version of Canada, there is uneasiness: how can we preserve the indefinable?

Ironically, the national predilection for trying to pinpoint who we are may be the secret of our success.

As Marshall McLuhan, writer and educator, once suggested, "Canada is the only country in the world that knows how to live without an identity." The truth is, we differ on what being Canadian means, but we live together anyway, and that may give us our quintessential "Canadian-ness."

COAST TO COAST Practically speaking, with more than 29.2 million Canadians scattered in pockets across the second largest country on earth, it's not surprising that there should be multiple versions of Canada. Most of the important touchstones of our identity – where we live, our ethnic background, our culture, our language, our religion and even our family lives – look different, depending where in the country we are.

On the East Coast, in the provinces of Nova Scotia, New Brunswick, Newfoundland and Prince Edward Island, much of the "old Canada" still survives amid the urban consumer culture of the 1990s. French and English ethnic groups predominate, primarily because most new arrivals to Canada don't settle on the East Coast (only 1.7% of foreign-born Canadians lived in Atlantic Canada in 1991). Many people live in smaller communities, often close to the sea. Prince Edward Island, Canada's smallest province, has the highest proportion of rural dwellers in Canada.

Throughout Atlantic Canada, and particularly in Newfoundland, communities that once depended on ocean harvests still reel from the closing of their fisheries. For many people on the East Coast, economic survival has long meant leaving home to find work in other parts of Canada.

Next door to the Atlantic provinces lies Quebec, the historic heart and soul of French Canada. Predominantly

Francophone – 82% of the population speak French as their mother tongue – the province also includes a long-standing English minority, despite a steady-but-slowing exodus of Anglophones. Fewer than one in ten Quebecers are immigrants to Canada, and the vast majority (88%) of this group make Montreal their home.

Quebec is a society in transition. Changing social mores are just part of the story. Nearly 86% of Quebec's population is Catholic (some six million Roman Catholics), but it would nonetheless appear many have chosen, for decades, to eschew the values of the Church. Quebec has the second lowest rate of first marriages (after the Northwest Territories) and the highest proportion of couples (almost one in five) living common-law in Canada. By 1990, almost half of all first-born children in Quebec were born out of wedlock.

Another province in transition is Ontario, the most populous province in the country. Like other Canadians, Ontarians are still dealing with the job losses, business closures and consumer uncertainty of the recession of the early 1990s. As inhabitants of the country's industrial and manufacturing heartland, southern Ontarians (along with their neighbours in Quebec) are adjusting to a new economic reality of free trade and globalization. Nevertheless, Ontario continues to attract the largest share of immigrants to Canada. Today, more than half of all immigrants in Canada live in Ontario.

In Manitoba, Saskatchewan and Alberta, the ethnic mix reflects waves of immigrants who began arriving from Western and Eastern Europe to settle on the prairies at the end of the 19th century. Manitoba is also home to about 50,000 Francophones, one of the larger French-speaking communities in Canada outside Quebec. Today, Alberta continues to be a fairly popular destination for Canadians moving west, while Saskatchewan's population has grown more slowly.

"**O**ut West," rural roots are still strong, but agricultural practices are changing, farms are becoming larger and more mechanized, and small family farms do not support today's standard of living. Fewer and fewer people now farm the land. The rural ghost towns of Saskatchewan stand as wistful symbols of the once-vibrant communities of a bygone era.

Canada's west coast and the mountain-sheltered city of Vancouver attract tens of thousands of people from across Canada and around the world each year, including a steady stream of retired Canadians and those lured by the milder winters. Recent immigrants from Hong Kong and other parts of Asia strengthen economic ties to prosperous Pacific Rim countries. By 1991, one out of every nine residents of British Columbia was of Asian origin.

Yukoners often refer to the rest of Canada as "the outside." Both the Northwest and Yukon territories have relatively tiny

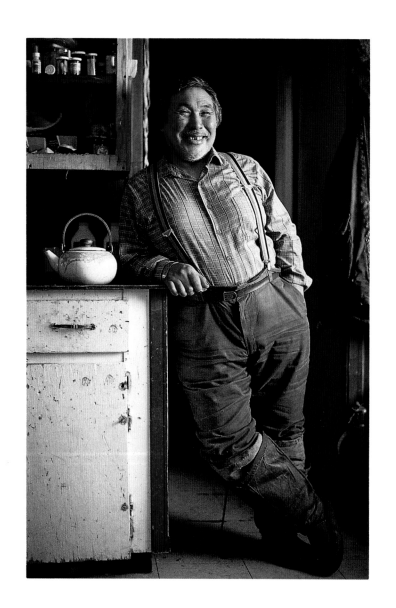

populations pocketed across vast landscapes. While 4% of Canadians report Aboriginal ancestry, almost half of those living up north have Aboriginal origins. Here, in the Northwest Territories, there are eight official languages: English, French, Chipewyan, Cree, Dogrib, Gwich'in, Inuktitut and Slavey.

Throughout the Canadian north, a culture has grown up which combines a distinct blend of frontier survivalism, Aboriginal traditions, and hefty doses of mainstream media and consumer goods imported from the south via airplane, boat, truck…and satellite dish.

GLOBAL GATHERING

With less than half of one percent of the world's population, Canada is a surprisingly global collective of 29.2 million people. Here, wealthy Hong Kong investors build malls in Vancouver suburbs, Somali refugees attend English-as-a-second-language classes in downtown Toronto, and descendants of Icelandic or Ukrainian or British settlers still carry on their cultures and traditions. The rising young Inuk singer, Susan Aglukark, performs a haunting rendition of the Canadian anthem…in Inuktitut.

Since the 1960s, the cultures of Canada have multiplied with a tide of newcomers from Asia and the Middle East, Africa, the Caribbean and Central and South America. Before 1961, nearly 90% of immigrants to Canada were from Europe.

Between 1981 and 1991, almost half came from Asia and the Middle East. Between 1989 and 1992, more than 150,000 people immigrated to Canada from Hong Kong and China. That's almost one out of every six immigrants.

With more ethnic groups sharing Canadian citizenship than ever before, old patterns of ethnicity have shifted. In 1991, people with either British (7.6 million) or French origins (6.2 million) still dominated, but the number of Canadians from other backgrounds had risen 34% from 1986.

Speaking of which…Immigration is changing how Canada sounds. Altogether, Canadians now speak more than 100 languages. The number of Canadians whose first language is neither French nor English rose by one million between 1981 and 1991 to 4.1 million.

But some language groups are so small they wouldn't fill a stand in the average hockey arena. Approximately 30 Aboriginal languages have fewer than 1,000 conversants including, for example, Mohawk (355), Okanagan (390), Kutchin (Loucheux)(430), Malecite (430), Kwakiutl (485), Coast Tsimshian (490) and Michif (840).

Other tiny language groups include those who speak some of the Celtic (265), Turkic (365), less common Asiatic (570) and Austro-Asiatic (675) languages, as well as those who speak Baluchi (70) and Byelorussian (535).

"KLAHOWYA TILLIKUMS" Although it sounds like an exotic foreign greeting, these are actually authentic Canadian words. "Klahowya Tillikums" is Chinook Jargon for "Hello, my friend." Like other pidgin languages, this Canadian West Coast pidgin was born along the trade routes of the 1830s, nurtured by settlers, traders and Aboriginals in need of a common tongue. By the turn of the century, more than 250,000 people spoke Chinook Jargon. Old-timer West Coast slang still includes some of the 700 words in its vocabulary, words such as "salt chuck" for the ocean and "high muckamucks" to describe the powerful and well-off.

Chinook Jargon flourished more than any other pidgin language in Canada, borrowing words from English, French and Aboriginal languages. Sometimes called "language still in its underwear," pidgin is one of three types of languages in Canada. The other two are the immigrant languages, including English and French, and Aboriginal languages.

In 1991, the Census found about 22.5 million people speaking English and 8.5 million speaking French. Other dominant languages were Italian, German and Chinese, with well over half a million people conversant in each language.

Immigration Since 1971, immigration has been an important part of population growth in Canada. This is because Canada's birth rate is fairly low: only 13.8 births per 1,000 in 1993.

Generally speaking, immigrants to Canada must meet specified criteria: those in the family class must have an extremely close relative living in Canada; independent class immigrants require certain levels of education, work experience and language ability; investors need to have a certain amount of money, and so on.

Investor immigrants have made the splashiest contribution. This group mushroomed from only 5 immigrants (not including dependents) in 1986 to 2,196 immigrants by 1992. Almost 90% of those who arrived in 1992 came from either Hong Kong or Taiwan.

These people are wealthy – their net worth must equal half a million dollars or more to enter Canada – and they must commit to investing in and creating jobs in Canada. Between 1989 and 1992, each investor brought or was prepared to bring an average of $2.3 million into Canada.

Canadians take pride in our international reputation for compassion and generosity. We have long had the highest refugee acceptance rate among all Organization for Economic Cooperation and Development (OECD) countries. Almost 42% of all those who applied for refugee status between

1989 and 1992 were accepted into Canada. In 1992, Canada welcomed 52,000 refugees.

After talking to Canadians about immigration – their hopes, desires, needs and concerns – the federal government announced a new immigration plan in late 1994. The plan marks a fundamental change in Canada's immigration policy. Among other things, the number of immigrants expected in 1995 will drop to between 190,000 and 215,000, from the planned level of 250,000 in 1994. Canada will also shift the balance of immigration toward more "economic" immigrants, including skilled workers and business people.

DRUMBEATS OF NATIONHOOD   The Aboriginal peoples were here long before European immigrants arrived to "found" Canada. But, despite their place in our history, we continue to face tough questions, at home and abroad, about their plight. In 1993, the Canadian Human Rights Commission deemed their situation "the most serious human rights problem in Canada."

Aboriginal communities cope with widespread unemployment, alcohol abuse and suicide. In 1991, the unemployment rate for Aboriginal people was 25%, more than double the national rate. In 1990, a staggering 29% of Aboriginal adults received social assistance, and the situation was even worse on reserves where the rate was 42%.

Although more than one million Canadians claim native ancestry, only 626,000 individuals identify themselves exclusively as members of the three Aboriginal groups recognized by the *Constitution Act, 1982*: (North American) Indian (460,680), Inuit (36,215) or Metis (135,265).

Among these groups, 171,000 people still speak one of the more than 50 remaining Aboriginal languages. About one in three North American Indian, Inuit and Metis adults can carry on a conversation in their native tongues, but only about one in five of their children can do so. The Inuit are the most fluent: 71% of adults and 64% of children can converse in Inuktitut.

Recognizing the plight many Aboriginals face, the Canadian government appointed the largest Royal Commission in Canadian history. The Royal Commission on Aboriginal Peoples is expected to report to Canadians about Aboriginal issues in 1995.

LIFE IS A HIGHWAY   To many, Canada conjures up images of wilderness, wildlife and plenty of snow. But our reputation as "hewers of wood and drawers of water" is out of date. Today, most of us live where the jobs are – about two-thirds of Canadians inhabit sprawling urban centres, living and working in a clutter of highrises, strip malls, connector roads and four-lane highways. By 1991, almost one in three Canadians lived in one of the country's three largest urban

centres: Toronto (pop. 4.3 million), Montreal (pop. 3.1 million) or Vancouver (pop. 1.6 million).

Some of this movement has been part of a long term shift from rural life, some of it the more immediate consequence of economic hard luck. The Grievous Angels, a Canadian rock band, tell a not unfamiliar story with their lyrics: "When the coal pits closed and our money ran low, we crossed the causeway into Ontario." Many Atlantic Canadians are moving west: over 39,000 left the East Coast in 1992. But in the same year, 32,000 Canadians relocated to the Atlantic provinces.

The influx of people to urban areas has moved the United Nations to call Toronto the most cosmopolitan city on earth. With more than one-third of all immigrants to Canada (70,000 to 80,000 people each year) settling here, the description would appear to fit. In 1991, there were about four million people in the Toronto region. By 2021, planners project the area will accommodate six million people, almost 15% of Canada's population focused in one large urban network.

THE GREY WAVE
Canada's face is wrinkling. Like all other industrialized countries, we are aging, as fewer babies are born and greater numbers of us live longer. More and more, older Canadians are dominating the population. In 1991, one Canadian in two was over 34. By 2036, three in five will be over 50 years old.

Great waves of Canadians have already hit old age and millions more are heading toward it. Since 1961, the number of seniors age 65 and over grew by 128%, from 1.4 million in 1961 to 3.2 million in 1991. Close behind are another 9.2 million baby boomers, many already having reached middle age. In the next forty years, boomers will help to almost triple the ranks of the elderly to 8.7 million.

An aging population holds profound implications for Canada. As the workforce "greys," the growing corps of retired Canadians will place pressure on public and private pension funds and savings plans. Younger working Canadians will be asked to support a generation of older people much larger than it is today. Eventually, the pool of candidates for physically demanding jobs such as construction, policing and fire fighting will shrink. Canadians will face important decisions in areas such as health care, social services and housing.

LOVE LIVES AND FAMILY STORIES
Canadians live together and love one another in so many different ways that often old assumptions about family no longer hold. While most Canadians (84%) still live in families, the fifties-style "traditional" family unit – mom at home, dad at work – has been replaced with a patchwork of creative living arrangements. Only about one in five Canadian families are so-called traditional earner families.

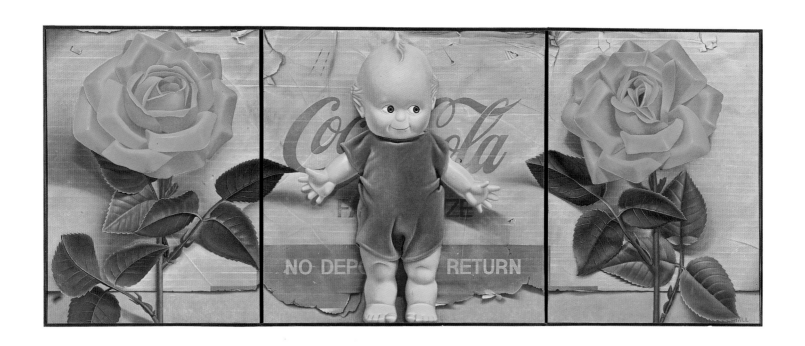

Today, married or common-law couples live together with or without children, lone parents raise children on their own, adult children may live with their parents, older relatives may move in with younger family members, and step or "blended" families create new family ties.

Divorce and...Re-marriage   Canada has one of the highest divorce rates in the world, although the United States still leads the way. In 1992, the divorce rate was 2.8 per 1,000 population, or about 79,000 Canadian couples splitting up. The American rate was 4.8 per 1,000 population. By 1991, there were almost one million lone-parent families in Canada (82% headed by women) largely due to divorce and separation.

The majority of lone-parent families (60%) headed by women lived below the low-income cut-off in 1993. In 1993, the average census family income for a lone-parent family headed by a woman was about $23,300.

Indeed, the situation for lone-parent families is so severe that governments have taken steps to remedy the situation. In Ontario, for example, there are about 62,000 registered cases of parents, usually fathers, not paying their child support – that's about half of all cases in that province. The federal and provincial governments have been cooperating to trace missing parents, garnishee wages, reclaim tax refunds or unemployment insurance payments, or repossess the property of parents who fail to pay child support. In future, governments may consider other options such as withholding drivers' licenses.

On the other hand, for many Canadians, marriage is an "if at first you don't succeed, try, try again" proposition. Since the early 1980s, almost one-third of all marriages have involved a partner who has been married before and who may already be a parent. In 1990, there were more than 340,000 "blended" families in Canada.

And No Marriage... An increasing number of Canadians skip the wedding altogether. The prevalence of Canadians getting married for the first time is shrinking – there's been a steadily declining number of marriages since 1972 – more Canadians are choosing to remain solo, and more Canadian couples are setting up house without getting married. The number of common-law couples doubled between 1981 and 1991. By 1991, 1.5 million Canadians (or 11.3% of all couples) were "living together."

Even today's parents are less likely to be married couples. By 1991, almost one of every ten families was headed by a couple living common-law. An increasing number of children are born out-of-wedlock. Unmarried women, including those who are divorced, separated, widowed and/or living common-law, gave birth to 26.3% of all children born in Canada in 1991, compared to less than 10% in 1977.

THE BALANCING ACT Working parents pay a price for making ends meet. Many report their stress levels are soaring, especially women. In a recent Statistics Canada survey, 34% of full-time working moms with children under 10 in dual-income families said they were "running on empty," while only 16% of their partners felt equally stressed. Juggling the demands of work and family has become a national preoccupation. Finding child care is often a crucial part of the balancing act. It has been estimated that 2.2 million Canadian children require child care. In 1991, however, the number of licensed daycare spaces was estimated at 330,000. Most parents rely on a network of neighbours, relatives and, in some cases, siblings. In 1988, almost one-quarter of children between the ages of 6 and 12 who needed care were latchkey kids, caring for themselves or being cared for by siblings.

In some cases, parents cope through work arrangements that include part-time, flextime, home-based, shift and weekend work. In 1988, almost 200,000 dual-earner couples reported deliberately "off-shifting," arranging their work schedules so that one parent could always be available to care for the kids.

Women's Work Changes in women's lives have helped change family life in Canada. By 1991, more than half of all adult women in Canada were in the labour market (six million women were either employed or officially looking for work).

ANGEL IN THE HOME Back in 1925, Agnes Macphail, a pioneer of women's rights in Canada, pointed out: "When I hear men talk about women being the angel of the home I always, mentally at least, shrug my shoulders in doubt." She suggested we might eventually "take turns at being angels."

But in 1992 women still spent twice as much time on being the "angel" of the home as did men. Women averaged 4.5 hours per day on child care, cooking and meal clean-up, house cleaning and laundry, shopping, maintenance and repairs, compared to 2.6 hours a day for men.

Among younger couples, however, change is afoot. Women under 35 still do the biggest share, but 13% report that their partners prepare meals, 16% say their partners do the dishes, and 15% report that their partners do laundry and housecleaning.

Agnes Macphail wanted more than equality in the home. In 1951, as a member of the Legislative Assembly of Ontario, she tabled groundbreaking equal pay legislation to ensure that women in that province were paid the same wage as men when they did the same job. In 1988, Ontario's new *Pay Equity Act* gave women the same pay as men in different jobs who perform work of equal value.

This is a 61% increase since 1976 (when less than four million women were in the labour force). Mothers with pre-schoolers have led the way: their participation rate increased 27% between 1976 and 1991.

Much of this is driven by economic necessity. In 1993, the average Canadian family had an income of $52,112, a decrease of slightly more than $800 (1.5%) since 1980. For all families, taxes now take a bigger bite. In 1992, families paid almost one-fifth (19.2%) of their income in federal and provincial taxes on average, compared to about 15% in 1971.

Dual-earner husband/wife families have the advantage: they averaged $75,700 in 1991, compared to $49,600 for single-earner families.

The Care Crunch As families get smaller and fewer women are available to stay home, there is no one to fulfil traditional care-giving roles. Although only a small number of seniors actually live with other family members (besides their spouses), some people fear a care crunch.

In 1990, Canada's "sandwich generation" – those with at least one child living at home and one parent over 65 – will include more than three million Canadians aged 35 to 65. By the year 2000, this group will have grown 30%.

In 1991, fewer than 10% of seniors lived in care-giving facilities. Depending on their circumstances, seniors who wish to remain independent may find that less traditional support, ranging from snow shovelling and other household maintenance to day programs, home-making services or subsidized apartments, is the key to their independence. Demands for these and other services are expected to escalate as the number of older Canadians rises and as the pool of caregivers becomes smaller.

GREAT EXPECTATIONS Change is everywhere in Canada, but our dreams about love and family still tend to be old-fashioned.

So-called "traditional" weddings, for example, stubbornly remain big business in Canada. But, despite the lavishness of such celebrations – *Wedding Bells* magazine suggests a typical wedding can cost as much as $10,000 – the high price of getting married is no insurance against divorce.

The reality is that living common-law has soared in popularity, divorce courts are bustling, an increasing number of Canadians may never marry, nevertheless most unmarried Canadians still expect to tie the knot. Young adults are particularly optimistic. According to Statistics Canada, 80% of Canadians aged 18 to 29 expect to marry. And they're right;

most of us do get married at least once, but today we are usually older than our parents were when they headed to the alter. By 1991, the average bride was about 27 years of age and the average groom was just under 29 years old. Thirty years ago, the average age for brides was 22 and grooms averaged 25.

Similarly old-fashioned expectations surround parenthood. Families are getting smaller and more couples are childless. The cost of raising children has skyrocketed – a Manitoba government estimate suggests raising a child to the age of 18 can cost more than $150,000. Yet most Canadians still expect to be parents. According to Statistics Canada, almost 90% of young Canadians aged 15 to 24 who do not yet have children expect to become parents in the future, and the majority plan to have at least two.

Family Feelings Canadians hold family close to their hearts. In a 1987 poll for *Maclean's* magazine, more than three-quarters of the respondents felt family was becoming either "more" or "much more" important to their lives, and about the same number ranked family as more important than either careers or religion.

A similar poll in 1994 found that we turn to our families for support, security and joy. More than half of us were happy with our families; the same number reported having had happy childhoods. Three-quarters of us said our families were full of love, and more than three-quarters of parents surveyed felt that having children had made them happier.

FAITH TO FAITH Our spiritual lives are changing. Christianity is still the principal religion (there were 12.3 million Catholics and 9.8 million Protestants in 1991). But there's been a dramatic drop – 1.2 million since 1981 – in the ranks of the four largest Protestant groups (United, Anglican, Presbyterian and Lutheran). As well, a smaller proportion of Canadians put their faith in formal religious institutions. In 1991, 3.3 million Canadians reported no religious affiliation, a 90% increase since 1981.

At the same time, some faiths experienced dramatic growth in the past decade. Small-but-blossoming Christian flocks include the Spiritualist (a 93% increase since 1981), Evangelical (76%), and Christian and Missionary Alliance (75%) congregations. Meanwhile, Asian immigrants have significantly upped the numbers of Buddhists, Hindus, Muslims and Sikhs in Canada. By 1991, these worshippers numbered 747,000, an increase of 144% since 1981.

Interestingly, despite the wave of popular interest in the "new

spirituality" – a phenomenon that has spawned numerous personalities, books, seminars and cassettes – most Canadians still tend to report their traditional religious affiliations. For example, only about 1,200 Canadians placed themselves in the "New Age" category in the 1991 Census.

ABOUT GIVING...

Canadians do believe in helping others. In 1938, the Newfoundland physician, Sir Wilfred Grenfell, pointed out that "the service we render to others is really the rent we pay for our room on this earth." In 1990, three-quarters of Canadians paid that rent by helping someone outside their own household with housework, chores, baby-sitting, drives, or giving money.

In 1993, more than 5 million Canadians donated $3.35 billion to charity. Despite economic worries, Canadians have managed to give a little more each year since 1984. In 1993, Canadian donors gave an average of $610 to help others. The older we were, the more we gave. In 1993, Canadian contributors aged 65 and over averaged $860 in gifts, compared to $310 for those under 35.

And, adding to our hectic schedules is volunteering. In 1987, more than five million Canadian adults gave more than 1 billion hours of time "free-of-charge" to help others. More than half of Canada's army of volunteers are women, and married women with jobs were at the front of the line.

CATHOLICS TO CONFUCIANS

Canadians practice almost 100 different types of religion including some as old as recorded history and others with hardly any history at all. Catholics and Protestants were by far the two largest religious groups in 1991, with 12.3 million Catholics and 9.8 million Protestants, representing about 80% of the population.

Yet some Canadians were observing Pagan rites dating back to pre-Christian times, while others were exploring the ancient Judaic mysticism of the Kabal religion. There were 3,200 Zoroastrians practicing pre-Islamic Persian beliefs, and 1,400 Jains conforming to an ancient Indian tradition. There were also 1,700 Taoists who followed the way of the Tao and 400 Confucians who aspired to the 2,500 year-old Chinese ideals of K'ung-fu-tzu (Confucius).

Statistics Canada also tells us that the New Age movement has especially strong appeal in Western Canada; among its 1,200 members, 60 % were women. Almost 3.3 million Canadians reported that they had no religious affiliation, including those who said they were Agnostics, Atheists or Free Thinkers.

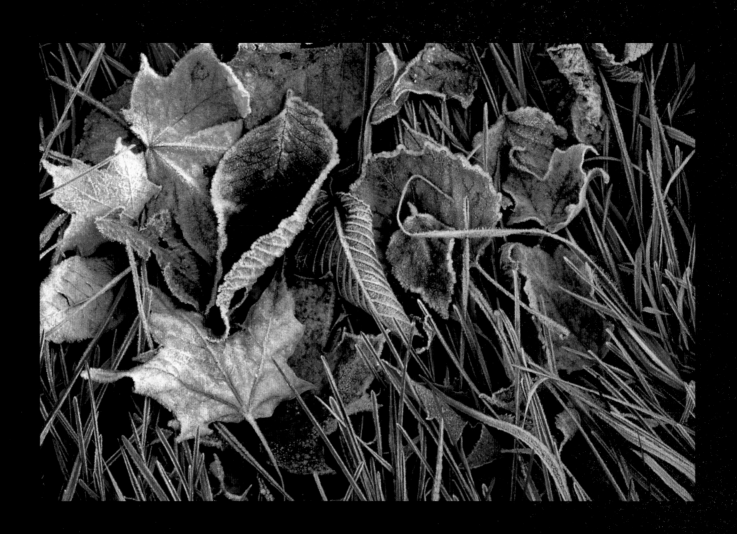

I came to Canada as a refugee. Forty-five years later, for me, Canada is a refuge still. It's a feeling that has been strengthened by decades of reporting on wars and other violence around the world. Sure, we have our problems, serious problems. But so far, we have avoided the plague of mass violence. Luck has had a hand in that, but, even more, so has Canadian restraint. From the FLQ crisis through Oka, events that elsewhere might have caused bloodbaths, we have managed not to let the bitterness of our divisions erode our humanity.

Joe Schlesinger. Journalist, foreign correspondent, author, Member of the Order of Canada.

In Prince Edward Island's old legislative buildings in Charlottetown, visitors encounter a bronze plaque. On it is written: "In the hearts and minds of the delegates who assembled in this room on September 1, 1864 was born the Dominion of Canada. Providence being their Guide, they builded better than they knew."

In fact, the political system Canada's founders created has proven itself tough and resilient. Based on principals of democracy and compassion, Canada has become one of the most respected nations of the world. Canadians today are better educated than previous generations, and healthier. We can expect to live longer. Our low crime rates are stable, or even dropping. We *can* say, with hindsight, that Canada's founders "builded better than they knew."

Yet like other nations we have our share of problems and troubling social issues. Polls find us with furrowed brow over the economy, the national debt and the current constitutional impasse. We also worry about violence in our society, and about the costs of our health care and education systems. But we also say, by a large majority, that we are satisfied with our lives and are proud to be Canadian.

The Debate Continues... While the Canadian constitution is physically a beautifully hand-written parchment stored in a climate-controlled room of the National Archives, legally and politically, it is a work-in-progress. Some might even say

it is a persisting argument, defining who we are as a people and what is the essence of our core. It began as the *British North America Act*, was renamed the *Constitution Act, 1867*, and has culminated, for the moment, in the *Canada Act of 1982* and the *Constitution Act, 1982*.

More than 128 years have passed since the constitution first became law, and during this time it has been amended many, many times. As voters' rejection of the 1992 Charlottetown Accord made plain, the tension of joining Canada's federal and provincial government systems, two systems of law and two official languages, is far from being fully resolved.

In the past decade, the most contentious issues have included Quebec's status within Confederation, the aspirations of Canada's Aboriginal peoples for self-government, re-distribution of federal and provincial powers, and reform of the Senate. Although a vigorous hybrid system has flourished since Confederation, debate is never far away.

Indeed, Canada's most recent constitutional stalemate set the stage for dramatic change in the fortunes of federal political parties. In October 1992, Canadians watched in stunned surprise as the governing Progressive Conservatives, led by Prime Minister Kim Campbell, were not just defeated but almost eliminated as a presence in the Canadian Parliament; the Conservatives dropped from 154 seats in the House of Commons to just two.

The New Democratic Party also suffered severe damage, losing all but nine of 43 seats. The Liberal Party won a commanding majority (177 seats), but their victories were concentrated in Ontario and the Atlantic Provinces.

In Quebec, the separatist Bloc Quebecois took 54 of 75 federal ridings – enough to make them the Official Opposition. The Reform Party dominated in British Columbia and Alberta and parts of Saskatchewan, winning 52 seats. Prior to the election, they had just one federal seat.

By late 1994, Quebec's status had again become the most pressing constitutional issue. On December 6, Quebec Premier Jacques Parizeau announced that his government intended to pass legislation declaring the province a sovereign country.

Quebec voters will be asked to approve this legislation sometime in 1995. As *Canada: A Portrait* went to press, forces on both sides of the sovereignty debate in Quebec were preparing for what will likely be a long and difficult struggle.

How Government Works   Over time, Canadians have come to expect government to embody the values we hold as a society – in particular, fairness and a willingness to help those in need.

Canada is one of a small number of nations offering its citizens universal health care, "cradle-to-grave" social security, and highly accessible education – but at a cost. In 1993-94, we spent an estimated $86 billion on social services – about $3,000 for every Canadian.

In large measure, these values are enshrined in the constitution, which sets out the basic structures framing Canada's system of law and justice. It is through our constitution that we have established federal and provincial governments, outlined their powers and the way they are elected. Through our constitution, we have set out the basic rights afforded to citizens of Canada and those we welcome into our country.

Canada is a constitutional monarchy, a confederation and a parliamentary democracy; it has two systems of civil law, the British common law and the French civil law, and two official languages, English and French. Legislative power is divided between Parliament and 10 provincial legislatures.

Canadians have lived under a monarchy since the first French regime in the 1600s. Canada's present Queen and head of state, Her Majesty Queen Elizabeth II of Great Britain, delegates her duties – largely ceremonial – to her representatives in Canada, the Governor General and the lieutenant governors. The Queen has representatives at both the federal and provincial level because Canada is a confederation.

Having a federal system of government means that law-

making authority in Canada is divided between the Parliament and the provincial legislatures, each having specific jurisdiction. At the federal level, legislative power is shared by the Senate and the House of Commons.

Federal power is divided among the government's legislative, executive and judicial branches. Elected representatives in the legislature adopt laws and vote on taxes and other administrative matters. The executive, consisting of the prime minister and Cabinet, proposes legislation, presents budgets to Parliament and implements laws. The judiciary is the final interpreter of these laws and regulations.

The Cabinet, headed by the prime minister, holds the government's actual authority. It varies in size depending on how many members the prime minister chooses; for example, numbering about 40 ministers under the last federal government, and 24 under the present one. The prime minister, who holds extensive powers, usually chooses cabinet ministers from among the governing party's elected members of Parliament, although senators may also be named to Cabinet.

The prime minister and the provincial premiers are, in principle, usually leaders of the political party that gained the largest number of seats in the legislature in the most recent election. There are exceptions. For instance, the Governor General or a lieutenant governor may ask the leader of a party with fewer seats to form a government if the incumbent government resigns.

Strictly speaking, the prime minister and Cabinet advise the Queen. Practically speaking, though, Cabinet holds the actual power, and the Governor General usually acts on Cabinet's advice.

Cabinet, which develops government policy, is responsible to Parliament's House of Commons. The Government of Canada, headed by Cabinet, performs its duties through federal departments, special boards and commissions and Crown corporations.

Provincial governments have a structure parallel to that of the federal government. Lieutenant governors represent the Queen in the provinces, each of which has a premier and a cabinet responsible for provincial departments, commissions and Crown corporations.

The Yukon and the Northwest Territories are special cases, and differ from provinces. Legislative assemblies govern the territories, and commissioners have duties similar to those of lieutenant governors, but they report to the minister of Indian Affairs and Northern Development, who has jurisdiction over the territories and Indian and Inuit affairs.

Municipal governments are created by the provinces to look after police and fire protection, local courts and jails, sanitation, snow removal and road maintenance.

Canada's *Charter* To protect civil liberties, the architects of Canada's Confederation followed Britain's example. They included safeguards established by the courts, and by landmark documents such as the British *Magna Carta*, in Canada's *Constitution Act, 1867*.

In 1982, the *Charter of Rights and Freedoms* was written into the *Constitution Act, 1982*. The *Charter* offers us freedoms and enshrines our rights. We have freedom of association and assembly, freedom of thought, conscience and religion, and freedom of the press.

We also have the right to vote in federal and provincial elections; the right to free movement within the country, language rights, equality rights; and legal guarantees such as the right to consult a lawyer, the right to a fair trial, the right to be presumed innocent until proven guilty, and the right to be protected against unreasonable searches, arbitrary imprisonment and cruel punishments. Special provisions also protect Native rights.

Perhaps Canada's most distinctive civil liberty is the right to speak and be understood in either official language – English or French – in all institutions of Parliament and the Government of Canada, including federal government departments and courtrooms. In fact, language rights are one of our oldest protected civil liberties, first enshrined in the *Constitution Act, 1867*.

THE MAPLE LEAF, FOREVER...In 1867, a Toronto school teacher composed the song "The Maple Leaf Forever." With its slow, almost monumental cadences, it became part of Canada's musical legacy, the incantation of school children and choirs across the land. But its subject, the maple leaf, had already found a place as a symbol of Canada.

In 1860, the maple leaf was adopted as our national emblem for use during the visit of the Prince of Wales and in 1914, Canadian soldiers used it on their military badges. Again, in 1939, Canada displayed it on naval and army equipment and on the regimental badges of its troops. But it was not until February 15, 1965 that the maple leaf took its place as the central motif of the Canadian flag. Indeed, Canada had not had its own national flag until that time, flying instead the Royal Union Flag and then the Canadian Red Ensign.

The new flag came into being only after a vigorous national debate focussed attention on the pressing need for a symbol of Canadian identity. It had been almost a hundred years since the creation of the song that would herald the place of the maple leaf in Canada's history...forever.

THE JUSTICE SYSTEM In 1993, Canada's overall crime rate dropped by 5% – the largest drop since Canadian crime statistics were first collected in 1962.

Still, many Canadians believe that increasing violence in our society has diminished our quality of life. We worry about youth crime, about violence generally, and about how effectively the justice system deals with offenders. We sign petitions, we come out for rallies, we appeal to our MPs and MLAs.

We Fear, But... Rates of police-reported violent crime in Canada stabilized in 1993 after ten years of steady increases averaging 5% per year. The bellwether of violent crime, experts tell us, is homicide. Homicides are carefully recorded; the numbers are reliable. In 1993, homicides declined by 14% to 630, the second decline in two years. Indeed, for almost a decade, Canada's rate of homicides per 100,000 population has hovered around the 2.5 mark – far below the 1975 peak of 3.0.

Three other categories of violent crime, from a total of six, also declined in 1993. Attempted murder declined by 6%, robbery by 10%, and abduction by 1%. The two types of violent crime that did increase in 1993 were assault, up 3%, and sexual assault, up 1%.

Youth Violence Still Rising In 1993, there was one police-reported violent youth crime for every 100 Canadian youth. Youth crime increased rapidly in the 1980s, climbing by 21% in 1989 alone. However, it increased by much less in 1993, by 6%. The large increases of the 1980s may have partly reflected society's decreased tolerance of violence – as in the Zero Tolerance policies of many school boards.

In 1993, one-half of young people charged with violent offences were charged with minor assaults, many of which may not have been considered serious enough to report a decade ago. Fewer youths were charged with property crimes in 1993 than in 1992: 11% fewer.

Crime Overview Canadians may worry about becoming victims of a violent crime, but we're much more likely to have our houses broken into or our cars stolen – both property crimes.

Of the almost three million *Criminal Code* incidents reported to police in Canada in 1993, 54% were property crimes, 11% were violent crimes, 7% were traffic offenses, and 28% were other offenses (including prostitution, arson and mischief). Youths aged 12 to 17 accounted for 22% of all persons charged, excluding *Criminal Code* traffic offenders.

For a decade, rates of property crime have climbed some years and dropped others, but remain little changed. In 1983, the rate per 100,000 Canadians was 5,589; ten years later, it was 5,562.

Not all categories of property crime have been this stable, however – the motor vehicle theft rate per 10,000 vehicles registered, for example, climbed 69% from 1983 to 1993.

Hidden Crimes... Police statistics track reported crime, but much crime – even violent crime – goes unreported. To get at this "hidden" crime, Statistics Canada in 1988 and again in 1993 asked 10,000 Canadians aged 15 and over about their experience with crime, and their perception of the risk crime poses. Respondents who had been victimized were asked if they had reported the crime to police.

In both years, a quarter of respondents had been victims of crime at least once. The highest rates per 1,000 people in 1993 were for assault (67) and theft of personal property (51). The highest rates per 1,000 households were for vandalism (55) and break and enter (50).

The stable rate of victimization was not reflected, however, in how people felt. Almost half felt that crime levels had gone up in their neighbourhoods. Yet the proportion who did not feel safe walking alone in their neighbourhoods at night changed little: 42% of women felt unsafe, and 10% of men.

Perhaps the most startling news is that nearly 90% of sexual assaults and 68% of ordinary assaults are not reported to police. In all crime categories, except breaking and entering, about half the crimes committed were not reported.

The System   Canada's criminal justice system includes the police, Crown prosecutors, the courts – which function in both civil and criminal matters – and penal institutions. The *Criminal Code* is the main body of law dealing with criminal offenses and legal procedures in Canada, but other important legislation includes the federal *Young Offenders Act,* the *Narcotic Control Act*, the *Food and Drug Act*, and provincial driving and liquor legislation.

Under the Canadian constitution, the federal government has the exclusive power to enact criminal law and establish criminal law procedures, while the provinces have responsibility for the administration of justice, including operating provincial courts of criminal jurisdiction.

The provinces operate prisons to incarcerate adult offenders receiving sentences of less than two years. The federal government operates penitentiaries for adult offenders sentenced to two-year or longer terms. Young offenders are normally sent to youth custody facilities or kept in "open custody" in group homes.

Civil law – which is concerned with individual and property rights and legal proceedings dealing with them – falls largely within the provinces' jurisdiction. Canada's civil law draws from two traditions. In most of Canada, it is based on the common law that originated in medieval England and evolved through judicial decisions. In Quebec, civil law is based on France's Napoleonic Code. A revised *Civil Code of the province of Québec* came into effect in 1994.

The Supreme Court of Canada, established in 1875, is the

highest court in the land, with jurisdiction in criminal and civil justice. Judges on the nine-member court are appointed by the Governor-in-Council, and may hold office until they retire at age 75.

The Enforcers   Canada's image abroad is of red-coated Mounties in wide Stetson hats astride horses. But today's Mountie is more likely to sit at a computer.

The Royal Canadian Mounted Police (RCMP) is Canada's national police force with approximately 14,000 peace officers and 7,100 civilian employees. It enforces many federal laws, particularly criminal and drug laws. It also represents Canada internationally as a member of the International Criminal Police Organization (INTERPOL).

The RCMP is the only force in the Yukon and the Northwest Territories. Eight provinces also contract with the RCMP to provide provincial police services in the smaller municipalities and in rural areas.

The RCMP has forensic laboratories across Canada, a computerized police information centre, the Canadian Police College in Ottawa and a training academy in Regina. The college offers advanced courses to members of other police forces in Canada and around the world.

Municipal police forces provide general police services in local areas. Where there is no municipal force, the federal or provincial police forces perform these duties.

PEACEFUL CANADA   Despite a common perception that our society is becoming more violent, most Canadians don't feel personally threatened by crime.

In its 1993 General Social Survey, Statistics Canada asked Canadians how they felt about their general level of safety from crime. It found a full 88% of Canadians were "very or somewhat satisfied." In contrast, only 11% of respondents said they were dissatisfied with their general level of safety. However, Canadians do feel a little edgy in specific situations, such as walking alone in their neighbourhoods after dark. The 1993 survey found 27% of Canadians feeling somewhat or very unsafe walking alone at night, while 72% said they felt safe.

For many Canadians, taking crime prevention steps has helped to enhance their peace of mind. Some 30% of respondents said their fears had led them to change their activities or avoid certain places, 32% installed new locks, 15% installed burglar alarms, 12% got a dog, 10% took a self defence course, 9% had their phone numbers changed and 2% obtained a gun.

Despite the common perception, overall crime rates in Canada are not increasing. In fact, Canada's overall crime rate actually fell by 5% in 1993, the largest drop since Canadian crime statistics were first collected three decades ago.

CANADA'S HEALTH Canadians' life expectancy at birth – 74.9 years for males and 81.2 years for females in 1992 – ranks among the world's longest. In 1991, 84% of Canadians were satisfied with their health. Four out of five elderly Canadians were very or rather satisfied with their health. In a 1991 special survey, Canada's adult Aboriginal population also overwhelmingly described their health as good, even while making it clear they had extensive problems.

Almost one-half of deaths in Canada each year are premature. The main culprits are six lifestyle factors: smoking, diet, elevated serum cholesterol, hypertension, diabetes and excessive alcohol use. Smoking accounts for half of all premature deaths in Canada.

Governments across Canada have in recent years focused on helping Canadians change their lifestyles to prevent illness and early death. The results so far have been encouraging – we're taking better care of ourselves.

For example, only about a quarter of men aged 15 and over smoked regularly in 1994, down from just over half in 1966. (The decrease for women was far less dramatic: 28% in 1966 versus 23% in 1994.) More Canadians are exercising regularly as well – 32% in 1991, up from 27% in 1985.

The System Canada's health care system is an interlocking set of ten provincial and two territorial systems. Each adheres to national standards, providing hospital and health services that are universal, publicly funded, comprehensive and accessible to all. Under the constitution, the provinces have jurisdiction over health services. The federal government shares health costs by transferring funds to the provinces according to a formula presently based on population. Health services for Canada's Aboriginal peoples are wholly paid for by the federal government.

Canadian governments spent an estimated $48 billion on health care in 1993-94 – almost $1,700 for each Canadian, second in the world after the United States. From 1981 to 1994, the proportion of Canada's Gross Domestic Product (GDP) spent on health care jumped from 7.5% to 10.1%.

In the 1990s, governments across Canada have been struggling to contain these rising health costs. Hospital beds are being eliminated and medical services capped or curtailed, and the federal government has appointed a national forum of experts and ordinary people to look for ways to fortify the nation's health while keeping costs in check.

The need for new approaches is pressing – Canada's population is aging, and the elderly account for a disproportionate share of health care costs. By the year 2036, three in five Canadians will be at least 50 years old. The seniors of today are generally healthly but a small number have chronic illnesses and need long-term care. By the age of 75, however, 90% of Canadians report at least one chronic health problem.

THE CHALLENGES OF DISABILITY Climbing stairs, tying shoe laces, preparing meals: most of us perform these daily activities without a second thought. But for the almost one in five Canadians with a disability, daily living can be a struggle.

In 1986, 13% of Canadians said they had one or more disabilities that interfered with their daily activities. By 1991, this had risen to 16% – about 4.2 million people. Why the increase? Partly it's the result of an aging population – almost half of Canadians aged 65 or older have disabilities, compared to only 14% of those aged 35 to 54. As well, Canadians may now be more willing to report a disability as awareness of the special needs of disabled people increases.

More than half of disabled Canadians in 1991 reported a mobility disability – difficulty walking, carrying an object for a short distance, or standing for long periods. Almost as many had problems with agility – the ability to bend over, dress themselves or grasp objects. About one in three had a hearing disability even when using a hearing aid, and 14% had sight problems that glasses or contact lenses could not correct.

Leading Causes of Death In 1992, cardiovascular disease and cancer together accounted for two-thirds of the almost 200,000 deaths in Canada. Cardiovascular disease has been the leading killer since early this century, but its proportion more than doubled from 1921 to 1961 – from about one in five deaths to just under half. Changing diets and improved medical treatment have brought the proportion down in recent decades to slightly less than four in ten.

Cancer has been the second leading cause of death for women since 1931 and for men since 1941. Unlike cardiovascular disease, though, cancer's share of all deaths has grown in recent years, particularly for men after age 55. The most common cancers for women are breast, lung and colorectal; for men, lung, prostate and colorectal cancers predominate.

Journey Risks Past age 30, our risk of dying within the next 12 months doubles every eight years. But what we're most likely to die from shifts as we age.

Canada's rate of infant mortality (death before age one) is among the lowest in the world, at 6.1 per 1,000 live births. However, the risk of infant death is still high relative to other ages. In 1981, a newborn baby was as likely to die over a 12 month period as was a 59 year old adult.

The main risk factors for infant death are low birth weight – closely linked to the mother's health and socio-economic status – and the mother's behaviour during pregnancy.

The risk of death from heart disease is low up to young adulthood – but then it climbs steadily. Prostate cancer begins to claim men after age 45; for women, breast cancer becomes a serious threat after 30. For most other major causes, such as motor vehicle accidents, the risk of death is relatively constant over a person's life span.

In the last 30 years in the United States and Canada, most of the declines in mortality and gains in life expectancy have been achieved in the elderly population – an unexpected and unexplained phenomenon. Once we have survived the perils of infancy, childhood and younger adulthood, our chances of living longer increase. At 65, life expectancy for females is another 20 years (for a total of 85), and for males it is 16 years (to 81 years). At 85, you are an even greater survivor, with a further life expectancy of 7 years for females (to 92) and 6 years for men (to 91). At these advanced ages, men and women have about the same life expectancies.

Healthy, Wealthy... Canadians may have equal access to health care, but they don't have equal access to health. The richest people in our communities are the healthiest, the middle income groups are somewhat less healthy, and the poor are even less so. They visit doctors most often.

In 1990, a health survey found that both education and income levels are faithfully mirrored in health data. More than one in three very poor persons (income of less than $10,000) reported fair or poor health, compared to one in 20 wealthy individuals (income of $60,000 or more).

There is also a life expectancy gap between the well-off and the "not-so." In 1986, life expectancy at birth for the poorest 20% of Canadians was almost four years lower than for the richest 20%. Higher smoking rates among the poor may account for up to a fifth of this gap.

A ground breaking 1991 Aboriginal Peoples Survey offers further evidence of the link between poverty and poor health. In 1990, more than half of Aboriginal Canadians had incomes below $10,000. Despite assertions in the survey that their health was good, one in three Aboriginals reported chronic health problems. Three-quarters had sought medical assistance in the 12 months before the interview, including about 5% who got help from a traditional healer. The most common illnesses were: arthritis/rheumatism (15%); high blood pressure (12%); bronchitis (9%); heart problems (7%) and diabetes (6%). About half felt that alcohol, drug abuse or family violence were problems in their communities.

EDUCATION   In the television commercial, a young man steps into a telephone booth, a newspaper folded under his arm. "Hi, I'm calling about your ad in the paper." A pause. "No, I don't have my high-school diploma. I understand, thanks anyways." He glances at his newspaper: he has crossed out

every help wanted ad. Angry and frustrated, he steps into a windy, rainy night.

Since 1992, television spots like this have helped make young Canadians aware of the bleak prospects facing high school drop-outs. A survey taken in 1991 found that drop-outs were more likely than graduates to be unemployed, working in blue collar or service jobs, or regular candidates for social assistance. Job prospects for drop-outs are simply dismal.

The message seems to be getting through – Canada's drop-out rate of 32% in 1991 was much less than the 1976 figure of 46%. Today only about one in three students leaves high school before graduating.

As well, drop-outs are increasingly likely to return to school. Drop-outs from earlier years made up a significant number of the 75,000 adults – mostly 34 years old and under – who in 1991 registered full-time at primary and secondary schools to finish their basic education.

Class Crowds   In the wake of Canada's post-1960s "baby bust," the number of young people is declining – yet full-time university enrolment increased by 50% between 1980 and 1992. More than a quarter of Canadian young people now go on to university level studies, compared to 16% in 1980.

Higher enrolment rates aren't the only factor boosting university populations – students are also spending more time in school. The average age for obtaining a bachelor degree is now around 26, two years later than a decade ago.

Class Honours   Canadians can take pride in having created one of the best endowed education systems in the world. In 1991, Canada was in first place among all OECD nations in per capita public spending on all levels of education combined, at 7.4% of GDP. In spending on post-secondary institutions, Canada was also number one, spending 2.6% of GDP, ahead of the U.S. at 2.4%. In 1991-92, government spending on education in Canada reached $53 billion – about 7.8% of GDP.

Total full-time enrolment in Canadian elementary, secondary and post-secondary institutions in 1992-93 was close to 6.2 million, with more than 5 million students in grade schools, 361,500 in community colleges and 569,000 at university.

The constitution gives the provinces exclusive responsibility for education, but the federal government funds the education of Indians on reserves, helps finance post-secondary education, and supports other educational activities.

Canadian schools offer education in three levels: elementary-secondary level (including pre-elementary); trade level, at both the elementary-secondary levels and post-secondary; and post-secondary level, consisting of community colleges (non-degree granting) and universities.

At the undergraduate level, universities had 496,917 full-time students in 1992-93, with graduate enrolment reaching 59,844. In 1992-93, Canadian universities granted 120,700 bachelor and first professional degrees and nearly 20,000 masters degrees and doctorates.

Change of Face In a remarkable turnabout, more Canadian women than men now walk the halls of academe. Yet women still tend to gravitate to "traditional" occupations, like teaching and nursing.

Through the 1980s, women played catch-up on university campuses, their numbers growing by 72% compared to 23% for men by 1992. In 1992, women received 57% of bachelor or first-level degrees and 48% of Masters degrees.

Women are chipping away at male bastions – often in large numbers, as in law, medicine and undergraduate math – but many disciplines, including engineering and the physical sciences, continue to be male dominated.

As well, in 1992-93, only 21% of university instructors were women – and female instructors are clustered in the lowest paying positions.

"A COOL CLEAN PLACE, is how she thinks of it, with a king and queen and Mounties wearing red jackets and people drinking tea and speaking to one another in polite tones, never mind that these images do not accord in any way with her real memories of the hurly-burly of that Winnipeg schoolyard and the dust and horse turds of Simcoe Street. It seemed to her that June day, as the train slid at last over the Michigan State line and entered Canada, that she had arrived at a healing kingdom."

Carol Shields, *The Stone Diaries*, 1993

*T*he marvellous thing about this country is that there is such a chance to discover who you are. We have big, blue open skies,

and the Prairies, and somehow that has given us an openness of spirit and a simplicity. We Canadians have heart.

As a dancer, I try to bring these qualities to my work. I try to be natural, committed and hard-working. In this way, I can bring

Canada to the world and to the people who come to see us dance.

Evelyn Hart, born in Toronto, Ontario. Resident guest artist with the Royal Winnipeg Ballet, Companion of the Order of Canada.

"**H**e Shoots! He Scores!" ran the ad in the sports section of the *Vancouver Sun*. But this time, it wasn't a hockey promotion. The Vancouver Opera was marketing *Don Giovanni* to sports fans. On the heels of an advertising campaign by the Vancouver Canucks headlined "The Opera It's Not," the Opera responded with a series of hockey one-liners for its productions. Spunky and robust, these good-natured campaigns raised the profile of both the Opera and the Canucks.

Hockey and opera are two of a dazzling array of leisure activities available to Canadians, and we've been spending more of our money on these activities during the last two decades, though the growth slowed slightly in the early 1980s and early 1990s. In 1992, we paid $34 billion for cultural and recreational goods and services – more than 8% of all consumer spending, and up from just over 6% in 1969.

But the rivalry between the Canucks and the Opera is a sign of today's energetic competition for the consumer – a truly daunting challenge given the wealth of entertainment opportunities we have and a population in a state of profound change. The growing cultural and ethnic diversity of the country is one of those changes: more than 30% of Canadians and almost 60% of Torontonians now report linguistic backgrounds other than English or French.

In 1992, Statistics Canada gave us a detailed picture of how Canadians 15 years and older use their leisure time. The Time Use Survey showed that we are busy, we have little time and there are many options available to us. Little wonder sports and cultural groups are in such dynamic pursuit of the modern consumer.

Over this rather urgent pursuit dances another player: the spectre of cutbacks in government funding. Many sports and cultural organizations have already felt the impact of the federal government's 10% reduction in grants and contributions initiated in 1993-94. The 1995 federal budget resulted in further cuts to bodies such as the Canadian Broadcasting Corporation (CBC), Telefilm Canada and the National Film Board as well as cuts in funding to 22 sports. More than ever, the interested consumer is becoming the lifeline of this industry.

COCOON UPDATE When Canadian playwright Sally Clark urged a friend to see her play at a Vancouver theatre, he exclaimed, "Oh, no, I couldn't do that! People my age rent videos and stay home with the baby."

Clark's friend may be one of the famed "cocooners," so-called for their tendency to curl up on the couch with a TV remote, or with all the new home entertaining options, he might have found a handy excuse not to go out. The fastest growing area of cultural spending is home entertainment equipment.

In 1992, the average family spent $186 on cable TV, up from $56 in 1982. More than 79% of households owned a VCR and 71% of us reported staying home to watch a movie while only 49% went out to the "flicks." In fact, there's been a steady decline in movie-going since the late 1980s.

Eight out of every ten Canadians listened to compact discs, cassettes or records in 1992, and in 1994, over 40% of Canadian homes had CD players. Games and hobby equipment cost us an average of $217 per household in 1992, and the 14.5% of households that purchased computers and related supplies spent an average $924.

So far, except for the drop in movie-going, the home entertainment explosion doesn't seem to have made a big dent in our "stepping out." But sports and cultural groups are keenly aware that the ever-present comforts of home beckon: powerful potential competition for the consumer's time and money.

SPOTLIGHT ON CONSUMERS Not only are we dealing with a home entertainment explosion, we're very different people than we once were – older, more culturally diverse, more educated, more likely to be in the workforce . . . *and* so busy that nearly 45% of us report cutting back on sleep to cope with all our obligations.

Of Age There are more than nine million baby boomers in Canada, born between 1946 and 1966, and together they represent one-third of the population. Now in their almost-30s to late-40s, the boomers are influencing trends just by their sheer numbers. No other age group attends performing arts events, visits museums or reads so frequently. But as they grow older, they may take after the current over-60s, whose attendance at performing arts and sports events, movie-going and museum visiting is lower than that of any other age group.

The challenge of the "greying" of Canada is toughest for sports and recreation groups because those activities traditionally attract young people. Only 25% of Canadians aged 55 and over regularly participate in amateur sport. Most of those who don't participate cite age and poor health as the reasons.

Meanwhile, younger Canadians are becoming yet another cultural force with which to contend. They account for much of the popularity of TV channels like MuchMusic, MusiquePlus and YTV and they're adept with computers, video games and VCRs.

And Differences Attracting new Canadians offers further challenges and opportunities. A sizeable portion of the population – about one in six – is made up of immigrants. Increasingly, people settling here arrive from Asia, the Caribbean, and Central and South America.

Those who are born here or who come from Europe or the United States attend the performing arts at similar rates, while those born elsewhere have a slightly lower attendance rate.

In 1992, Statistics Canada found that immigrants from Asia and Central and South America spend a great deal more on home entertainment equipment than do people born in the U.S. and Europe, and somewhat more than the Canadian-born.

Time nor money One or both seem to be in short supply in recent years. There are more single-parent families, more unemployed people, and more people just "out of time" in Canada. When one-third of us report feeling constantly under stress juggling all the demands on our time, chances are we're too exhausted for a football game or symphony concert.

And money does matter because the wealthier we are, the more likely we'll attend the performing arts. In 1992, 58% of Canadians with household incomes over $80,000 went "out to the theatre" compared with only 28% of those with incomes between $30,000 and $40,000.

The well-to-do were also more active in sports, which often requires paying for equipment, coaching, and facilities. In households with annual incomes of $80,000 or more, 63% took part in amateur sport, versus only 31% of those whose income was below $20,000.

Education The level of schooling we've attained also makes a difference. In 1992, 41% of Canadians with at least some post-secondary education attended the performing arts, but that number dropped to 19% for those of us with less education. The comparable figures for professional sporting events were 38% and 24%.

SPOTLIGHT ON CULTURE Directly employing 461,000 workers, from jazz musicians to movie producers to educators, the culture industry is a significant and growing economic force in Canada. In fact, since the 1970s, the cultural labour force has actually grown at a much faster rate than the overall labour force and the population itself.

In 1992, the arts and cultural industries made up 2.7% of Canada's Gross Domestic Product (GDP). That comes to $15.9 billion. This includes the unpaid work of many thousands of volunteers who raise money for their local theatre or conduct tours of historic sites. In 1992-93, in heritage institutions alone, over 54,000 of us worked as volunteers.

HERITAGE INSIGHTS The vigour of the Canadian cultural enterprise has taken hold only recently. While a few Canadian museums trace their roots to before Confederation, it wasn't until 1947 that the Canadian Museums Association was formed. By 1992-93, Statistics Canada's survey of heritage institutions encompassed over 2,200 organizations, ranging from archives, art galleries and museums to arboretums, aquariums, historic sites, nature parks, observatories, planetariums and zoos.

JUST HUMMING When Canadian artist Bryan Adams titled his 1991 hit single "Can't Stop This Thing We Started," he could easily have been referring to the Canadian music scene.

Canadians are showing a voracious appetite for "home-grown" talent. In 1993-94, sales of recordings with Canadian content topped $92 million, up 30% over the previous year. Overall, Canadian content selections accounted for nearly 13% of the recording industry's national sales in 1993-94, up from only 8% just four years earlier.

As sales have soared, so too have the number of new releases. In 1993-94, 719 new Canadian content recordings – including albums by such popular performers as Sloan, the Crash Test Dummies, Sarah McLachlan and Beau Dommage – were released in Canada, up 7.5% from the previous year. New releases of non-Canadian content rose by less than 1%.

To be classified as a Canadian content selection, a recording must meet any two of the following criteria, as set out by the Canadian Radio-Television and Telecommunications Commission (CRTC): the music must be composed by a Canadian, the instrumentation or lyrics must be principally performed by a Canadian, the live performance must be wholly recorded in Canada, the lyrics must be written by a Canadian.

Institutions with large collections, splendid buildings, and internationally respected exhibitions, like the Royal Ontario Museum in Toronto, the University of British Columbia's Museum of Anthropology, and the Museum of Fine Arts in Montreal, welcome visitors from Canada and abroad. So do Canada's 23 sports museums and halls of fame, 26 botanical gardens, and nearly 700 community museums, some no larger than a room.

Canadians are devotees of their heritage institutions: there were more than 54 million visits to heritage institutions and an additional 53.9 million to nature parks in 1992-93. In the same period, some 32% of Canadians aged 15 and over reported going to a museum. People in Nova Scotia are particularly keen about historic sites: a higher proportion of Nova Scotians, 37%, visited such sites than did any other Canadians.

Popular as heritage institutions are, attendance declined in 1992-93, though less dramatically than the previous year. Dynamic new approaches to attracting consumers have resulted in an extended museum landscape, with interactive computer games, multimedia presentations, and new community-oriented programs and exhibitions.

Blockbuster shows, those with immense popular appeal and energetic marketing strategies, are part of the arsenal. The Art Gallery of Ontario's Barnes Exhibit of 1994 was a historic coup. With its 83 rare paintings by such masters as Cézanne, Matisse, Renoir and Picasso, it attracted nearly 600,000 visitors, about 60% of them from outside Metropolitan Toronto.

ON STAGE In 1957, when Parliament established the Canada Council to support the arts, there were four professional theatre companies in the country. Many amateur groups performed on makeshift stages in garages and barns. Outside the largest centres, music was mostly performed in auditoriums and school gymnasiums barely dry from the sweat of that day's basketball game.

Only 36 years later, Statistics Canada's 1992-93 survey of the professional performing arts counted 273 theatre companies, nearly 100 music organizations, 51 dance companies and 13 opera companies. In only a generation's time, most of Canada's professional performing arts groups were born, grew up, and reached maturity.

Today, you can watch a Canadian play in Corner Brook, Newfoundland, and in Whitehorse in the Yukon. You can listen to Bach and Beethoven in Chicoutimi, Saint John and Kelowna. In Vancouver, Winnipeg, Toronto and Montreal, you can experience Canada's renowned ballet and modern dance companies. Audiences abroad thrill to the voluptuous energy of cutting-edge dance companies like O Vertigo Danse, the soaring music of the Montreal Symphony Orchestra, the

brilliant clarity of Toronto's Tafelmusik Baroque Orchestra and the intensity of the Green Thumb Theatre troupe of Vancouver.

Nonetheless, art groups have not been immune to tough times. In 1992-93, the 435 companies responding to Statistics Canada's survey gave more than 39,000 performances before a total audience of some 13.9 million. Just over 30% of Canadians reported attending a performing arts event in 1992: that's 6.4 million people, easily surpassing the 5 million who went to popular music concerts.

Buoyant as these numbers are, however these companies haven't matched the all-time high of nearly 15 million spectators they achieved in 1988-89. This is an especially pressing concern since performance companies earn, on average, 50% of their income and rely on government grants and private funding for the balance. The principal manner of earning income is through ticket sales. As a result, performing arts companies are courting consumers with a wide range of innovative measures: discounts, instalment payment plans, flexible subscription packages, two shows for the cost of one, and "pay what you can" matinees.

But especially in Toronto, performing arts blockbusters, commercially produced mega-musicals like *Cats*, *Les Misérables*, *The Phantom of the Opera* and *Show Boat*, draw phenomenal crowds. In late 1994, *Phantom* celebrated its

fifth anniversary in Toronto, having given a record-breaking 2,095 performances after selling 4.2 million tickets.

Although these shows provide employment for Canadian actors, dancers, designers, musicians and technical staff, most of their material originates abroad.

Artists energetically debate whether such productions stimulate interest in all the arts or simply drain audiences from the not-for-profit companies, which produce a high calibre of Canadian work.

In 1992-93, 66% of performances were Canadian content. Opera companies performed 4% Canadian works, music organizations 21%, theatres 72%, and dance companies 78%.

Music On the popular music front, Canadians sell well on the international market. Major artists like Bryan Adams, Celine Dion, k.d. lang, Loreena McKennitt and Roch Voisine continue their success across the globe, and newer artists like the Holly Cole Trio, who's a hit in Japan, are also making a name for themselves abroad.

Kashtin, a top Canadian Aboriginal band from the Maliotenam reserve outside Sept-Îles on Quebec's north shore, recently released a debut album for Sony Music. Kashtin sings in Innu, a language understood by about 10,000 people in the world, but the group has already sold more than 350,000 copies of its first two independent albums.

THE WRITTEN WORD Canadians relish reading. More Canadians (7.2 million in all) borrow books from libraries than visit museums, attend the performing arts, or go to professional sports events. Among our leisure activities at home, reading is one of the most popular, with 92% of us enjoying newspapers, 80% magazines and 66% books. If we live in British Columbia, we're among the most devoted readers in the country: in 1992, 88% of British Columbians reported reading magazines and 78% read books.

Books Canada's book publishers produce everything from drama, fiction, non-fiction and poetry to educational and scholarly material in both English and French. Some firms also publish in other languages. In 1992-93, there were 323 publishing firms in Canada, each with revenues over $50,000, an increase of 37 firms from 1987-88. Together the firms published more than 9,000 books, 19% more than five years earlier.

Canadian-authored titles accounted for over 71% of the books. Sales of books in and outside Canada, including publishers' own titles and those sold by 44 exclusive agents marketing works by other firms, totalled almost $1.5 billion.

Foreign sales and exports have been rising for some years and went from just over $226 million in 1991-92 to $274 million the next year, in good part because of the strong showing of French-language firms on the international market. But the

increase in sales in Canada was surprisingly modest, given that Canadians are reading more. It may be that we're stretching our reading dollars by borrowing books instead of buying them.

Periodicals   Their names form a tapestry of the Canadian landscape: there's *Prairie Fire* in Winnipeg, *The Fiddlehead* in Fredericton, *Estuaire* in Montreal, *Grain* in Regina, *Brick* in Toronto and *Up Here* in Yellowknife. Colourful as they are, Canadian literary magazines are one of the least visible cultural products in the country. Few newsstands stock more than a handful, accounting for only 14% of newsstand sales. **I**n 1992-93, more than 1,400 periodicals were published in Canada, with total revenues of $852 million. Consumer magazines, over 550 in all, reflect the wide and eclectic tastes of Canadians; well-known general interest magazines like *L'actualité*, *Canadian Living*, *Chatelaine* and *Maclean's* are big sellers. There are also magazines about the arts, business, the environment, gardening, health, parenting, politics, religion, sports, travel, and a number of popular titles for children like *Chickadee*, *Les Débrouillards*, *Owl* and *Vidéo-Presse*.

But Canada's magazines are going through troubled times. In 1992-93, revenues from advertising were at a five-year low. Circulation declined by 4% and a number of consumer magazines ceased publication. Nonetheless, by cutting costs,

SANDY BAR

Came across a place that harbours
Pioneers of Sandy Bar;
Harbours long departed heroes,
Heroes now of Sandy Bar.

Penned by Guttormur J. Guttormsson, Canadian-born son of an Icelandic homesteader, these words echo across Sandy Bar, gravesite of the first pioneers in the Icelandic River district. Guttormsson was born in 1878 near Riverton, Manitoba and his celebrated poetry pays tribute to those Icelanders who settled the Argyle and lakehead area of his province during the 1800s. The rich, vibrant literary tradition of the Icelanders, like that of other immigrants to Canada, is part of our national poetry and folklore.

reducing staff and raising prices, the industry managed to increase overall profits from the slim rates of recent years.

Like books and other cultural products, periodicals must compete for their share of the domestic market with foreign products, especially from the United States, which benefit from economies of scale impossible in the smaller Canadian market. More than 60 U.S. magazines have a paid circulation in Canada of over 25,000, and they continue to dominate sales.

BROADCASTING   Turn on the TV and, depending where you are in Canada, you'll probably find 30 to 40 cable channels, maybe half a dozen of them Canadian. Of that half dozen, most will be airing an American program. From the outset of Canadian television, the big challenge for our broadcasters has been Canadians' love affair with American programs. We enjoy our *Seinfelds*, *Frasiers* and *America's Funniest Home Videos*.

We're next door to Hollywood, and we can buy successful American programs for a fraction of what they cost to make in the United States. Once on screen in Canada, they deliver large audiences to advertisers and hence large revenues to broadcasters.

On the other hand, producing original drama and comedy in Canada for a limited domestic market is very expensive; by some estimates 10 times more costly than buying from foreign suppliers. It's no wonder that almost 75% of what English-speaking Canadians watch originates outside Canada, predominantly in the U.S. But reports indicate that Canadians want it all: we don't want to relinquish our foreign programs, but we want to watch Canadian shows too.

The second challenge for network broadcasting is our formidable geography: Cape Spear, Newfoundland, is closer to Ireland than to Winnipeg, Canada.

The story is very different for French-speaking Canadians. Prompted by their strong interest in watching French-language programs, they tune in by the millions to made-in-Quebec dramas and comedies, and they've succeeded in making popular media stars of their TV performers. Foreign programs account for just 35% of their viewing.

Air "Traffic"   The Canadian broadcasting industry is made up of private and public broadcasters in radio and TV. Private television comprises networks such as CTV (in English) and TVA (in French), private affiliates of the CBC, and a number of independent stations. In 1993, excluding the CBC, Canada's licensed and operating stations included 219 television stations, 644 AM radio stations, and 346 FM stations. In 1993, radio and television broadcasting revenues as a whole totalled $2.5 billion, and the total revenues for the cable TV industry were $2 billion. But privately owned radio and television showed stunningly different financial results. After some years of economic difficulty, private TV reported a resounding profit of $58.5 million, up from under $30 million just a year earlier. Private radio, on the other hand, posted a net loss of $48.2 million in 1993.

Sales of air time, largely for advertising commercials, are the bread and butter of the broadcasting industry, accounting for almost 92% of revenues. For the industry as a whole, these sales decreased nearly 3% in 1993, but the drop was sharper for radio, which lost 3.7%. The CBC experienced a precipitous 8.7% decline.

The future of conventional television remains insecure. First of all, Canadians are watching less TV than they once did, and the decline is led by teenagers and young children. Their "television time" has dropped more than three hours a week since 1986. And because we have more and more channels available, audiences are fragmenting and advertising revenues falling. Pay and specialty channels, first introduced in Canada in the 1980s, now account for over 10% of our viewing time, and VCRs take up another 5%.

THE CBC It may be that warm, raspy voice of Peter Gzowski welcoming us to his electronic hearth every weekday morning on CBC English radio's *Morningside*. It may be the next "can't miss" episode of *La Petite Vie*, CBC French

television's hilarious comedy series seen by a record-breaking 86% of the francophone audience at the beginning of 1995. For millions of Canadians, programs like these *are* the CBC, proof that it remains a powerful instrument for culture, communication and identity in our country.

Created by Parliament in 1936, the CBC broadcasts across six time zones, reaching about 99% of Canadians. It operates major national television networks in both English and French and four radio networks, two in each official language. And it operates two specialty news networks and Radio Canada International.

That's no small task, and it costs money. For 1993-94, the CBC's total operating expenses after taxes were $1.48 billion. About 72 cents of each dollar of its income came from the federal government, another 22 cents from advertising and the balance from subscription fees for CBC Newsworld and its French counterpart, *Réseau de l'information*.

In a typical week, 6.6 million (31% of the population 15 years and older) report listening to CBC radio and, of these, 1.5 million listen for 10 or more hours. CBC television draws 79% of Canadians for at least some viewing each week, and 3.6 million of us watch it for 10 hours or more.

But the French TV network has been more successful than the English in finding a distinctive voice and a wide following among its audience. It pioneered the now-famous

téléroman, serial dramas depicting the past and present-day life of ordinary people, some of them running as long as seven years, drawing millions of viewers every week.

In the last few years, the CBC's major objective has been to create an English TV schedule that is unmistakably Canadian and distinct from the largely American material offered by private broadcasters. By 1993-94, nearly 90% of the CBC's prime-time programming was Canadian, and the full schedule had reached 65% Canadian content.

FILM AND VIDEO

Director Ted Kotcheff once said, "Financing a film in Canada is like trying to juggle a watermelon, a peach, and a pea at the same time. Just when you think you've got them all up in the air, the pea slips through your fingers."

In the high-risk world of Canadian filmmaking, you can't afford to fumble. You need lots of capital from many sources: pre-sales and advances from distributors, broadcast license fees for TV productions, money from private investors, joint ventures and co-production agreements, and financial assistance from public agencies at various levels of government. Minus any one of them, and your film probably won't get made.

Yet there's no doubt that film and television production is one of the fastest growing fields in the culture industry. In 1992-93, Canada had 667 film and video production companies, making everything from commercials and industrial training films to documentaries, experimental films, full-length features and television series. Their overall profitability has improved, with their average profit margin jumping to 8.7% in 1992-93 from a ten-year low of 1.5% just two years earlier.

International Acclaim

Many Canadians seldom see Canadian feature films, since finding them at your neighbourhood theatre or video store is still not easy. Canadian features account for only 5.2% of theatrical distribution revenues, in part because of a high degree of foreign control of distribution.

But more and more Canadian features are winning popular and critical acclaim here and abroad. Denys Arcand's *The Decline of the American Empire* showed the world the quality of Quebec filmmaking, winning the 1986 International Critics Prize at the Cannes Film Festival. Repeating Arcand's success, this time with a Toronto story, was Atom Egoyan's *Exotica*, which took the 1994 Cannes International Critics Prize and the award for best Canadian feature at the Toronto International Film Festival.

Canadian producers are successfully exploiting the home entertainment market. In 1992-93, 138 producers were active in conventional and pay TV production, compared to only 86 four years earlier. And the share of film distribution revenues

generated by foreign-controlled companies in the home entertainment market has fallen significantly, from 55.0% in 1987-88 to 38.9% in 1992-93.

Sandra Macdonald, president of the Canadian Film and Television Production Association, points out that "Canadians have had more success getting into American television than any other country does." Shows like *Kids in the Hall*, the Degrassi Street series, and *Anne of Green Gables* have drawn large audiences in the United States, and the TV series *Blanche* has already been sold to 10 countries.

Canada has signed more than 23 co-production treaties with other nations. Allowing film and TV productions to qualify as domestic content in the treaty countries makes it possible to get financial support in both nations. Between 1991-92 and 1992-93, total budgets for Canadian television co-productions increased 214%, and foreign investment in feature film co-productions tripled.

TEAM SPIRIT In Canada, sports and fitness are big business. There's scarcely a community in the country that doesn't offer its inhabitants the chance to bowl, curl, skate, play basketball and hockey, and more. There are over three million Canadians playing competitive sport in clubs, teams and leagues. There are some 10,000 to 15,000 amateur players identified provincially or nationally as "high performance"

athletes. In any one year, 2,000 to 3,000 are eligible to compete individually or as members of Canada's national teams in international games and world championships.

Some 15 million Canadians over age 10 take part in physical activity at least every other day for 30 minutes or more, about half of them energetically enough to improve their cardiovascular health. In 1991, Statistics Canada found that some 32% of Canadian adults consider themselves "very active" in recreational activity compared with 27% in 1985.

At the time of the last Census (1991), about 53,000 Canadians worked in sports and recreation, up from just over 46,000 five years earlier. From 1971 to 1986, the number of women in these jobs quadrupled, while the number of men doubled. But paid professionals are just part of the team. The amateur coaching network is largely volunteer-based, with fewer than 1% of the estimated 400,000 coaches being full-time professionals. It's estimated that nearly 1.5 million Canadians work without pay in sports and recreation.

Bleacher Stats Some 6.7 million Canadians reported going to a professional sports event in 1992 – that's slightly more than attended the performing arts and slightly fewer than visited museums – and 9.6 million of us said we participated in amateur sport. Far more men than women are sports spectators and active in sport.

But the most important influence on our participation seems

" *Dear* monsieur eaton, would you be so kind as to send me a canadiens' hockey sweater
for my son, roch, who is ten years old and a little bit tall for his age?"
– ROCH CARRIER, *THE HOCKEY SWEATER*

to be our earlier experiences in organized school sport. Over half the adults who took part in school sports remain regular participants, compared with only 37% of those who did not. Canadians whose mother tongue is neither English nor French have a lower participation rate in amateur sports (36%) than either Francophones (49%) or Anglophones (47%).

Sporting Chances   Canada, home to Terry Fox and Rick Hansen, is a fitting leader in advancing the cause of disabled athletes. We have been instrumental in establishing the International Paralympic Committee, which organizes Paralympics and multi-disability world games and championships. In 1992, Canada hosted its first Winter Games for disabled athletes. In the same year, at the Summer Paralympics, Canadian athletes won 75 medals. Since the inception of Winter Paralympics, Canadians have been particularly successful in alpine events, in which 40 of their 47 medals have been won.

But the 1994 Commonwealth Games, held in Victoria, were the first international games in which athletes with disabilities were full team members, officially acknowledged as competitors with their awards counting in a country's medal ledger. Canada finished these games in second place overall, with a total of 128 medals. Two of the forty Canadian golds were contributed by disabled athletes, swimmer Andrew Haley and Jeff Adams, who won the 800-metre wheelchair race.

CANADA'S ATHLETES OF THE YEAR   Every year Canadian Press, Canada's largest news wire service, recognizes Canada's athletic *crème de la crème* with the Athlete of the Year awards. In 1994, the female winner was biathlete Myriam Bédard, the first Canadian woman ever to win two gold medals at a Winter Olympics (Lillehammer, 1994). The male winner was figure skater Elvis Stojko, flamboyant silver medalist at Lillehammer. The athletes chosen the most often, between the years 1932 and 1994, were Wayne Gretzky (hockey) and Marlene Stewart-Street (golf): 5 times each.

Previous winners include: 1993 – Kate Pace (skiing), Mario Lemieux (hockey); 1992 – Silken Laumann (rowing), Mark Tewksbury (swimming); 1991– Silken Laumann (rowing), Kurt Browning (figure skating); 1990 – Helen Kelesi (tennis), Kurt Browning (figure skating); 1989 – Helen Kelesi (tennis), Wayne Gretzky (hockey); 1988 – Carolyn Waldo (synchronized swimming), Mario Lemieux (hockey); 1987 – Carolyn Waldo (synchronized swimming), Ben Johnson (track and field); 1986 – Laurie Graham (skiing), Ben Johnson (track and field); 1985 – Carling Bassett (tennis), Wayne Gretzky (hockey); 1984 – Sylvie Bernier (diving), Alex Bauman (swimming); 1983 – Carling Basset (tennis), Wayne Gretzky (hockey); 1982 – Gerry Sorenson (skiing), Wayne Gretzky (hockey).

WORLD STAGE, INK. A small village in the Italian Alps, seemingly frozen in time. Bombay, India during the political Emergency of the early 1970s. A bombed-out chalet near Naples in the twilight of World War II.

What do these exotic settings have in common? All are featured in novels that have recently won Canada's top award for fiction, the Governor General's Literary Award. The writers of these books have made all the world their stage – and the world has embraced their efforts.

In 1992, Sri Lankan-born Michael Ondaatje's Governor General winner, *The English Patient*, was also co-winner of Britain's prestigious Booker Prize, awarded annually to the best novel published in the Commonwealth. Carol Shields, 1993 Governor General winner for *The Stone Diaries*, became in 1994 the first Canadian-born writer to also win the Pulitzer Prize for Fiction, the most prestigious literary award in the United States (Shields holds both Canadian and American citizenship).

Nor does the list stop here. Antonine Maillet, another recipient of the Governor General's Literary award, Gabrielle Roy, Margaret Atwood, Robertson Davies and Yves Beauchemin have all drawn the international spotlight. In 1990, Yves Beauchemin won the *Prix du grand public du Salon du Livre de Montréal* and the French prize, *le prix Jean-Giono*, for his novel, *Juliette Pomerleau*.

The Canadian sports landscape is changing in other ways. Soccer is a case in point. With 20 million games played across the globe each year, it's one of the most popular sports in the world, but traditionally of little interest in North America. That's changing here. The number of registered players in Canada rose from 200,000 in 1982 to 350,000, 12 years later.

In many sports, women are becoming far more active. The Canadian Sport Council reports that women's hockey is one of the fastest growing sports in the country, and girls are enrolling in soccer in the same numbers as boys, while new club registrations for rowing are split equally between the two sexes.

Striking Gold The men and women in red and white always thrill Canadians with their grace and courage in international competition. In 1992, Canadians won more medals at the Winter Olympics in Albertville, France, than at any other Olympics since 1932. In the 1992 Barcelona Summer Olympics, Canada almost doubled its winnings from Seoul, South Korea, four years earlier. The eyes of the world were on Canadian Silken Laumann, who had suffered a terrible leg injury only ten weeks before the Games but went on to take a bronze medal in rowing. In fact, rowing was the theme of many Canadian successes at Barcelona, accounting for four of our six gold medals.

In 1993, Canadians brought home more world titles than ever

before. At the World Figure Skating Championships, Isabelle Brasseur and Lloyd Eisler captured the gold in the pairs division and Kurt Browning won his fourth world championship. On the slopes, Kate Pace was crowned 1993 Alpine Ski Champion in downhill. Nathalie Lambert, two-time Overall World Cup Champion in short track speed skating, collected seven gold medals. At only 21 years of age, Jean-Luc Brassard captured virtually every title available in freestyle skiing.

But the biggest news of 1993 actually belonged to 1992. Sylvie "Strikes Gold!" roared the headlines across the country when, in December 1993, the International Olympics Committee awarded a belated gold medal to Sylvie Fréchette for her stunning performance in solo synchronized swimming at the Barcelona Olympics.

Then came 1994 and Lillehammer. Canadians were considered a sure bet to beat our previous performance standards, and so we did, winning more medals and top-eight finishes than any other Canadian Winter Olympic team. Biathlete Myriam Bédard became the first woman and only the second Canadian ever to win two gold medals in a single Winter Olympics, and Jean-Luc Brassard once again won gold in men's freestyle moguls. Taking a silver medal at the Olympics and the 1994 world title in figure skating, Elvis Stojko combined his martial arts training and skating grace in a demonstration of the poetry of power.

EXCERPT FROM A SPEECH given by HRH Queen Elizabeth II on the occasion of a state dinner during the XV Commonwealth Games in Victoria, British Columbia, on August 18, 1994.

" Today in sport, athletes are achieving standards of excellence which would have been deemed impossible only a few years ago – Canadians are no strangers to these standards. For example, track and field performances by such Canadian legends as Percy Williams and Fanny Rosenfeld at the 1928 Olympics were not equalled until the 1960s, when British Columbian Harry Jerome tied the world record for the 100-metre run. Such accomplishments still stand as milestones in Canadian track and field.

Today, one can name Canadian heroes and heroines among those who meet those impossibly high standards – 'Man in Motion' wheelchair athlete Rick Hansen; figure skater Kurt Browning; track and field athlete Angela Chalmers; synchronized swimmer Sylvie Fréchette; decathlete Michael Smith; canoeist Alwyn Morris; and rower Silken Laumann, to name only a few.

Participation and personal dedication to doing one's best, however, are equally important accomplishments. As Rick Hansen said in 1986: 'You have to be the best you can be with what you have.'"

*I*n January 1992, I answered a newspaper ad for a job as a Canadian astronaut. Six months later, after a rigorous selection

process, I was selected into the 8-member astronaut corps and granted the privilege of representing Canada in space. This is

a most uncommon and challenging opportunity, but it is also a way to contribute back to a country that has given me so much.

For Canada is a country of unlimited possibilities, a country that has allowed me the freedom to try to be whatever I wanted to

be. In Canada, anyone can set goals and fulfil dreams. And that is indeed, its true beauty.

Julie Payette, born in Montreal, Quebec. Engineer and Canadian astronaut currently training to represent Canada in space flight.

THE ECONOMY

It's 7:00 a.m. on a February Monday, 1995. In downtown Montreal, an alarm clock rings. Within minutes the house is alive with the smells of cooking (bacon from a farm north of Edmonton, coffee from Brazil) and the electronic trill of a telephone manufactured in southern Ontario. Soon the couple, a tax lawyer and her sales manager husband, are out the door and into their car, which has been assembled near Montreal from Australian and Mexican parts.

More than 400 years ago, in 1535, French explorer Jacques Cartier gazed from a hilltop at the site where this house now stands. He described the scene like this:

"It (is) fine land with large fields covered with corn...in the middle of these fields stands the village of Hochelaga."

If Cartier were able to return today to the hilltop he named Mount Royal, he would view a vista of malls, hospitals, freeways, office towers and high-rises. In the city's countless shops he would be able to buy a vast range of goods made in Canada and imported from around the world. He would be able to transmit news of his discoveries to France in a split second. Around him he would hear French, English and many other languages spoken.

Canada has come a remarkable distance in her relatively young life. First a colonial outpost, trading on furs and timber and other abundant natural resources, Canada has built one of the most diverse and productive economies in the world.

Annual growth of the Gross Domestic Product (GDP), which is the measure of the value of all goods and services produced in our economy, averaged 5.2% through the 1950s and 1960s, 4.7% in the 1970s and 3.1% in the 1980s. Today, Canada's GDP has one of the fastest rates of growth of the major industrialized countries.

Indeed, Canada's economy ranks seventh largest among these countries and Canadians are among the wealthiest people on earth, with per capita GDP in 1994 of C$20,420, compared to the Americans, at US$20,844. This economic strength has allowed us to develop social programs and services that rank among the best in the world.

Yet, like other countries, we face a number of economic problems. Individual and regional disparities persist. Government debt is at record levels and unemployment remains high.

Despite these difficulties, which have been made more acute by the recession of the early 1990s, Canada is well-positioned to build on its many economic strengths. These include a highly skilled and educated workforce, a thriving export sector, and strength in both the resource industries and manufacturing.

ECONOMIC NEWSCAPERS? Picking up a newspaper or a magazine in 1991 or 1992 probably meant encountering such alarming headlines as: HIGH

UNEMPLOYMENT HERE TO STAY. THE JOBLESS RECOVERY. MANUFACTURING DOWN FOR THE COUNT?

According to stories like these, old economic rules and loyalties were becoming obsolete; a new world had emerged in which people and companies from every nation were buying, selling and investing wherever it made the most sense. Businesses were operating in a radical new way, with new production techniques, and changing relationships with employees, suppliers and customers.

Some of the popular thinking of the day had it that the automotive, mining and forestry industries would soon take a back seat to high-tech industries; that high paying, full-time jobs would be displaced by new technology; that unemployment would remain chronically above 10%; and that many laid-off workers would never be recalled, as manufacturing plants closed their gates forever.

But much of this has not happened. While Canada's recovery from the recession that began in 1990 was unusually slow, by early 1994 economic growth was up and running both in Canada and throughout the major industrialized countries.

Canadian companies were creating full-time jobs at a breakthrough pace and investing heavily in new machinery and equipment. Canadian timber, minerals and other natural resources were fetching top dollar. Manufacturers were producing more than ever before, and unemployment was once again below 10% while inflation was apparently down for the count.

Yet Canada's economy is changing – but slowly. For decades, we have been shifting from a natural resource-based economy towards a "white collar" or service economy. In the early 1960s, about five out of ten Canadian workers were employed in manufacturing, construction or natural resource industries. By 1994, less than three out of ten were working in these areas.

From 1976 to 1994, the service sector produced most of Canada's new employment. The number of service jobs grew by 55%, or 3.5 million jobs, while employment in the goods-producing sector expanded by only 2%.

Service jobs tend to be more secure than goods-producing jobs. This is because service industries are less affected by cycles of economic growth and recession than are goods-producing industries, in part because consumers need many services – such as health care and education – in bad times as well as good.

On the other hand, service jobs pay on average only about 72% of what goods-producing jobs pay. As well, service jobs average less than 30 hours per week, compared to about 40 hours for goods-producing jobs. Not surprisingly then, two of the three highest paying industries in Canada are goods-producing: mining and forestry.

WHO WORKS? Who works in Canada has changed as much as what we work at. From 1976 to 1994, the proportion of Canadian women either working or looking for work climbed from 46% to 58%, while the proportion of men dropped slightly, from 78% to 73%. Overall, that meant that the proportion of Canadian adults in the labour force climbed from 61% to 66%.

Canada hasn't been able to create jobs fast enough to keep up with the growing labour force since the 1960s. Partly as a result, our unemployment rate has risen steadily.

In 1969, the rate was 4.4%. Ten years later, it had climbed to 7.4%. During the 1981-82 recession, it peaked at 12.8%, dropping to 7.5% in 1988. In late 1990, it again began to climb, reaching 11.9% in November 1992. In late 1994, the rate fell below 10% for the first time in almost three years. With so many Canadians out of work, wage freezes and cuts have been common in the 1990s, even in union contracts.

A SHRINKING PAYCHEQUE For the 84% of Canadians who live in families, the best way to track our progress in the standard-of-living sweepstakes is family income. Since peaking in 1989, average family income for census families had dropped 7.0% by 1993 — the longest and steepest decline since the end of World War II.

Two key trends have affected the fortune of families since the

CATCHING UP Canadian women have traditionally earned less than men. In 1993, Canadian women earned 72% of what men did, virtually unchanged from the previous year. The gap had narrowed suddenly by 2% in 1991 after years of slow improvement.

But women who weren't in the workforce just a few years ago are jumping right over the gender gap. In 1993, working women aged 15 to 24 earned 91% as much as men the same age. Women over 55 earned only 70% as much as men their age.

A BUCKET AND A MOP How much is housework worth? According to Statistics Canada, the answer is $13,340 a year. That's how much it would cost an average Canadian household to pay someone to do laundry, house-cleaning, gardening, caregiving and shopping. At that rate, housework weighs in at equivalent to 41% of Canada's GDP.

Statistics Canada calculates that children, especially small ones, add considerably to the bill. People with one or more children under five years of age spent 920 hours a year on domestic work in 1992, and an extra 790 hours a year per child in caregiving activities. Households with no children under 19 spent 776 hours a year on domestic work. Women put in 66% of the time spent on housework.

late seventies – the holding pattern for men's incomes and the flood of women into the labour force. Today, if the Joneses want to do as well as they did in the sixties, Mrs. Jones probably has to work outside the home.

Since 1980, the gender gap in earnings has closed significantly. Women have made moderate gains while men saw no real gains. In 1993, women employed full time earned an annual average of $28,392, about 72% of men's annual average of $39,433. In 1980, women earned about 64% of what men did.

Lone-parent families headed by women have traditionally had a hard time of it. In the past decade or so their income has remained fairly stable, from an average income of $22,665 in 1980 to $22,621 in 1993. Male lone-parent families, a tiny minority among families (1%), averaged about $34,556 in 1993, less than the $35,810 they earned in 1980.

As Canadians age, they tend to earn more. In 1993, couples under 45 with children averaged $54,545, while couples aged 45 and older averaged $66,696. This gap between younger and older seems to be widening. In 1980, the younger families earned 10% less than the older families. By 1993, this had increased to 18%.

NINE–TO–FIVE?

Traditionally, life in Canada was centred around the 40-hour work week. Today Canadians are working a week that's much longer than 40 hours…or a lot shorter.

In 1989, almost 25% of full-time workers averaged more than 40 hours a week, up from 17% in 1981. Many of these over-timers are in jobs that pay better and require more education. While the number of Canadian workers on this treadmill may be rising, so is the part-time workforce – those who work fewer than 30 hours a week. About 17% of all Canadian jobs are now part-time, up from 14% in 1981. Part-time work suits most, but in 1993 one in three such workers told Statistics Canada they would prefer a full-time job. Some were working on contracts or other temporary arrangements; some 70% were women.

"LESS IS A POSSIBILITY"

Canadian novelist Douglas Coupland's 1992 bestseller *Generation X* gave voice to a disenfranchised generation – those born too late to catch the magic bus to Woodstock and the prosperity of the 1960s and 1970s.

Coupland's twenty-something characters don't have careers, they have McJobs, which he describes as, "Low-pay, low-prestige, low-dignity, low-benefit, no-future jobs in the service sector." McJobs also tend to be part-time and here today, gone tomorrow. And here, at the bottom of the earnings scale, Coupland's fiction meets the statistics…and they agree.

From 1991 to 1994, the unemployment rate for those aged 15 to 24 was five to seven percentage points higher than the national average.

Generally though, lower-paid workers have always tended to be younger and less educated than better-paid workers, but during the 1960s and 1970s, the earnings gap between the two groups was stable. Then, during the recession of the early 1980s, the earnings gap started to widen noticeably.

By 1989, men at the bottom of the earnings scale earned 8.4% less, adjusted for inflation, than they did in 1981. Meanwhile, men in the middle of the scale lost 0.1%, while top-earning men gained 5.5%. Women with regular full-time jobs had a similar experience – those at the low end lost 3%, those in the middle gained 3.4%, and those at the high end gained 7.8%. Canada's youngest workers bore the brunt of the pay cuts – for example, men aged 17 to 24 earned 18% less in 1988 than in 1981. Younger workers also had much higher unemployment rates than older workers, and the trend continued through the latest recession.

MYTH BUSTERS The recession of the early 1990s – the second in 10 years – was particularly worrisome to Canadians because it appeared to coincide with profound changes in how Western economies function. As manufacturing plants closed and retail firms went bankrupt,

THE 1% CLUB It has no private golf course, tennis courts or even official membership card. But it could be one of Canada's most exclusive demographic clubs.

We are referring, of course, to the wealthiest 1% of Canadian families, measured by their average income – $295,300 in 1991. That's more than five times what the average Canadian family earned. The 73,600 families in the 1% club are big investors. In 1990, they made 10 times as much as the average Canadian family from investments. Through the 1980s, their incomes grew more than for average Canadians; 16% for club members and 9% for non-members.

laying off hundreds of workers nationwide, we quickly became used to a new language of anxiety, featuring words like "downsizing," "restructuring" and "rationalizing." Many wondered if Canada's future was to be merely more of the same.

But then everything changed. In mid-1993, Canada's GDP began to climb markedly, driven by manufacturing in Ontario and Quebec and some resource industries in Alberta and British Columbia. By year's end, GDP had grown 2.6% – and the recovery was still gathering steam. In 1994, GDP grew 4.2%, creating about 400,000 jobs, mostly full-time, and pushing unemployment below 10% for the first time in almost three years. Once again, Canada's economy was booming.

Yet what was new about this recession was that it lasted a long, long time. In the 1981-82 recession, GDP fell 5% but returned to its pre-recession level in nine months. In 1990, GDP fell 3% but took 32 months to recover. Employment recovered even more slowly, taking 50 months, versus 36 months in 1982. Until the end of 1994, unemployment remained higher than 10%, far above the pre-recession low of 7.5%.

RECOVERY STARS Although the hardest-hit sector of the recession was manufacturing, reports of its demise were greatly exaggerated. While output dropped 13% between 1989 and late 1991, this sector shot back to life in 1992, growing 15% by the end of 1994 at about equal rates each year.

The key to this growth was a rising demand for Canadian exports. In 1994, exports made up half of Canada's manufacturing output, a significant change from almost 40% just three years earlier. Machinery and equipment (which includes electrical products) surpassed the value of automotive products for the first time ever in 1994 – and this despite a 44% growth in automotive exports over 1993.

Yet almost half of manufacturing industries (accounting for close to half of output) have so far failed to recover. When free trade with the United States began in 1988, industries like clothing, footwear, leather products, furniture, and printing and publishing became vulnerable to U.S. imports. They were also unequipped to sell their wares in the highly competitive U.S. market. On the other hand, some industries that *have* had this savvy, including non-automotive transportation equipment (such as buses and trains), are also failing to recover.

RESOURCE BOOM Electrical products played a key role in the recovery – which would seem to support the popular belief that high-tech is the wave of the future. But in fact, most of the top-performing manufacturing industries in the recovery were Canada's traditional leaders – motor

COLLAR BLUES Canada's latest recession was largely blue-collar. Between 1990 and 1992, 71% of jobs lost were blue-collar, mostly in goods-producing industries. The good news was reserved for white-collar managers, most in service industries: their unemployment rate ranged from 3.3% to 6.1% – far lower than the overall rate.

I GIVE UP Canada's unemployment rate doesn't account for the so-called "hidden unemployed" – those who would like to work but have stopped searching because they believe no work is available. In 1992, about 550,000 Canadians found themselves in this group.

vehicles, wood, paper, smelting, and refining and related industries.

Canada's loggers and miners have been putting in overtime because of a great demand for lumber, aluminum, copper, pulp, oil, natural gas, wheat and other resource products. By December 1994, prices for these products had risen about 15% over the previous 12 months, the strongest increase since the early 1980s. And employment climbed 10% in resource industries in the same year – compared to 5% in manufacturing.

In 1994, British Columbia and Alberta led Canada in job creation; employment was up 31% in mining and 9% in forestry. In Central Canada, job growth was steady thanks to the manufacturing export boom.

JOBS, JOBS, JOBS Where GDP goes, employment tends to follow. In 1994, Canada's economy created close to 400,000 jobs, twice that of 1993. Yet unemployment persists for certain groups and regions.

In 1994, the unemployment rate for workers aged 15 to 24 was 16.5%, compared to a national rate of 10.4%. Newfoundland's rate was twice the national rate and Prince Edward Island fared only slightly better.

No matter where you lived in Canada, replacing a lost job became increasingly more difficult in the 1990s. In 1989, the average unemployed person could expect to spend almost 18 weeks on a job hunt before finding work. By 1994, this had grown to 26 weeks.

Unemployment statistics don't tell the whole story, however. Many unemployed don't qualify for unemployment insurance because they have recently been self-employed or are attending school, or they are 65 or older. Many others are still unemployed after their period of benefits ends. In 1993, about 623,000 Canadians fell into these categories – more than during the shorter, more intense recession of the early 1980s.

A Statistics Canada survey showed that a fraction of firms account for a disproportionate share of total unemployment insurance benefits paid. Between 1986 and 1990, the study found that layoffs by the same 12% of firms accounted for 40% of all benefits paid. These firms employed only 14% of Canada's workforce and represent all sectors of the economy but are concentrated in construction and the less dynamic service industries.

THE STRUCTURE Every day thousands of decisions, regulations and financial transactions shape Canada's economic life. Four major players drive this activity: business, including the financial sector, consumers, government and Canada's trade partners.

Business Canadians run more than a million businesses, ranging from the corner grocery store to corporations that may employ thousands of people. Collectively, these businesses employ the majority of Canada's workforce, organize the production of goods and services and take the risks (and profits) that go hand in hand with business enterprise.

Business investment creates jobs and fuels economic growth. However, this investment is highly volatile, influenced by consumer demand, interest rates and economic prospects. For example, business plant and equipment investment dropped from 12.8% of GDP in 1990 to 9.8% in 1994. That was a difference of several billion dollars in the wake of the recession.

The Financial Sector At the heart of Canada's economic life is its financial sector. Canada's domestic and foreign chartered banks are the country's largest financial institutions, financing business start-ups and expansions and helping consumers buy goods.

In early 1995, Canada's banking system consisted of 9 Canadian-owned banks controlling total worldwide assets valued at $777.1 billion. Fifty-one foreign-owned banks controlled total assets valued at $64.9 billion.

As well as borrowing from banks, Canada's businesses raise capital in Canada's bond markets. Corporations issued about $10.8 billion in bonds in 1994, while the provinces and the federal government issued about $83 billion in bonds in 1993-94. In 1994, the value of shares traded on the Toronto

and Montreal stock exchanges, far and away the largest of Canada's five stock exchanges, was about $215 billion.

Consumers Whatever else we may be as individuals – mothers, fathers, sons or daughters – Canadians are consumers. As we shop in supermarkets, department stores and other businesses, our changing tastes and priorities determine what businesses produce, where they locate, and how they develop over time. In 1994, Canadian consumers spent about $454 billion – equivalent to nearly three-quarters of GDP, or about $15,700 each.

As consumers, we are highly sensitive to changes in the economy. Rising unemployment or interest rates, new or increased taxes – all of these can dampen our spending on all but essential goods and services. During the recent recovery, we were unusually cautious about making the big-ticket purchases – houses, cars and major appliances – that are a traditional sign of a recovery. By early 1994, however, we were again in the spending mood, and consumer spending had climbed 7% by the end of the year.

The Government Canada's federal government plays a lead role in managing the national economy. It influences Canada's interest and exchange rates through the Bank of Canada, regulates industry and trade, sets tax rates, and with the provinces helps fund the basic services, such as education and health care, that support Canadian society. Federal and provincial governments also build roads, bridges, airports and other infrastructure underpinning Canada's economic development.

Many government departments and agencies – notably the National Research Council and Industry Canada – conduct and fund research and development that helps Canadian industry become more competitive. Information collected by Statistics Canada is used to calculate the national unemployment rate, GDP and the inflation rate – essential economic indicators.

Governments also provide essential services that the private market cannot perform profitably, such as ferry services in remote areas. Often government business enterprises – which behave much like private sector companies but are responsible to Parliament or provincial legislatures – provide these services. In 1993, there were 141 federal and 337 provincial government business enterprises, employing almost 300,000 Canadians.

Governments at all levels use tax revenues to support the disabled, the chronically ill, the unemployed, the elderly, and others in need. More than half of Canada's tax revenue goes to individual Canadians through programs such as veterans' benefits, unemployment insurance payments and family allowances.

The federal government also redistributes resources among

the provinces and territories. Federal taxation revenues collected in the more prosperous provinces such as Ontario, British Columbia and Alberta are transferred to less prosperous provinces such as Quebec and the Maritime Provinces. These transfers ensure that all Canadians, regardless of their income or where they live, have access to comparable health care, education and other government services.

The wide range of services Canada's governments deliver come at a price. In 1994, total government taxation revenue amounted to more than $235 billion – just over $9,000 for every Canadian.

Besides influencing Canada's overall economic environment, governments have an immense direct effect on spending and employment. In 1993, Canada's municipal, provincial and federal governments spent about $355 billion – equal to almost 68% of total GDP. In 1994, government employed some 2.1 million Canadians – about 16.5% of the total work force.

Trade Partners Canada sells more than a quarter of its goods and services abroad, and imports commodities and manufactured goods from around the world.

Traditionally, Canada has exported natural resources and imported manufactured goods. Because of our small population, other countries have been able to produce manufactured goods in larger quantities, and more cheaply. The United States has a more mature manufacturing sector with a larger population to which it can sell, and thus is much less reliant on exports than Canada.

Natural resources are still important to Canada's trade – accounting for about 31% of total exports in 1994 – but we now have a diverse non-resource manufacturing sector, responsible in 1994 for 45% of exports.

Canada and the U.S. share the largest two-way trade in the world. Three-quarters of Canada's exports go to the U.S., and the U.S. in turn supplies three-quarters of Canada's imports. Canada's other important trading partners are Japan, the United Kingdom, Germany, China and Mexico. Several large trade deals signed with Canada in the autumn of 1994 will strengthen China's position.

Canada imports mostly manufactured end products – machinery and equipment, electronic goods, computers and consumer items. In 1994, Canada ran a trade deficit in end products of $29 billion.

TAX BITE In Canada, the government pays many of its bills by taxing our income. In 1994-95, personal income tax accounted for 47% of federal revenues, up from 39% in 1974-75. The contribution of corporate income tax dropped from 16% to 8%.

We paid more in unemployment insurance contributions, which more than doubled from 6% of total revenues in 1974-75 to 14% in 1994-95. The Goods and Services Tax, which didn't exist in 1974-75, contributed 14% of federal revenue in 1994-95.

The big-ticket federal government expense is social services. In 1994-95, these services consumed 33% of the federal budget. Interest charges on the federal debt followed at 25%, then protection of persons and property at 9%.

For two decades, social services and interest charges on the debt have been taking ever larger slices of the government expenditure pie. In 1994-95, these two accounted for almost 60% of federal expenditures, up from 42% in 1974-75.

Of course, the provinces and territories also take in revenue, chiefly from personal income taxes (estimated to be 26% of the total in 1994-95), general sales taxes (13%) and transfers from the federal government (19%). These revenues pay for health care (26% of the total in 1994-95), education (18%) and social services (19%).

DEBT LOAD Canada's federal, provincial and municipal governments have not broken even – that is, collected as much in taxes as they've spent – since 1974. By early 1995, federal government debt had reached $543 billion – almost $19,000 for every Canadian. Annual deficits have steadily increased provincial and territorial government debt, which had reached $181.7 billion by early 1995.

How did the debt load get so large? From 1965 to 1990, government revenues increased an average of 11.8% every year – but spending climbed 12.3%. By 1994-95, the gap between what the federal government takes in and what it pays was estimated to have been $39.3 billion. The gap for the provinces and territories was $20.0 billion.

Reducing these annual deficits, and eventually eliminating accumulated debt, has become a critical target for governments across Canada. High debt loads reduce the amount governments can spend on programs, and make it difficult to borrow additional money at favourable interest rates.

In early 1995, the federal government responded to these pressures by introducing a budget calling for unprecedented cuts in government expenditures, coupled with modest tax increases. Over three years some 45,000 civil servants, 14% of the total, will be laid off, and transfers of revenue to the provinces will decline substantially. Some subsidies to western farmers and businesses will be eliminated, along with many other kinds of government support.

Yet even with a much leaner government, a balanced federal budget is still a distant goal.

The government hopes to cut its annual deficit from $37.9 billion in 1994-95 to $24.3 billion in 1996-97 – bringing the accumulated federal debt to more than $600 billion. Canadians are unlikely to begin paying down this debt until early in the next century.

THE BANK OF CANADA

Although the Bank of Canada – the government's central bank – isn't in the RRSP or mortgage business, it *does* affect every Canadian. As an agent of government, the Bank of Canada controls Canada's supply of money and credit, and thus affects levels of spending and economic activity.

The bank implements monetary policy through its control of the money supply – the cash and liquid deposits held by Canadian households. The bank exercises its control primarily through the chartered banks.

Every week, the bank sets the "bank rate" (the rate at which it is willing to lend money to the commercial banks), which in turn affects the interest rates that Canada's commercial banks charge businesses and individuals.

The Bank of Canada's interest rate policies can have a major impact on inflation, which occurs when prices rise, causing the relative value of money to fall. Inflation can slow economic growth as the unpredictability of future prices may cause businesses to shy away from long-term investments.

INTEREST RATES AND INFLATION

Canada's interest rates have fluctuated dramatically in recent decades. A quick survey of five-year intervals makes this plain: on November 12, 1970, the rate was 6.00%; on September 3, 1975, it was 9.00%; by December 31, 1980, it had climbed to a near-record 17.26%, but by December 25, 1985 it had dropped to 9.49%. Recently, the rate has been at its lowest level in 30 years, dropping to 3.87% in February of 1994.

The inflation rate – as measured by the Consumer Price Index – also rises and falls unpredictably. The lowest annual average increase since 1955 was 0.2% in 1994; the highest was 12.4% in 1981. Throughout 1993 and 1994, Canada's inflation rate remained below 2%.

NOTICE TO PURCHASERS

In the sale of all livestock and produce, Kitchener Stock Yards Co. Limited acts as agent only.

No warranty expressed or implied is given by the agent. Livestock or Produce becomes the property and responsibility of the Purchaser as soon as declared sold. Any dispute is between buyer and seller. Health of animals shall be determined

*I*was born on Turtle Island (North America as the colonists say) in what is now called Canada, our home and native land. As an actor representing Canada, I take great pride in calling my home, my home. As I travel around the world, I realize how far we humans have come and how little distance we have attained.

Through it all, mother earth sustains, living under the weight of her bickering children. Through it all, I take great comfort in knowing that no matter where I go, I can click my heels three times and say, "There's no place like home."

Graham Greene, born on the Six Nations of the Grand River, Ontario. Canadian actor, Genie and Oscar nominee.

Canada is probably the best country in which to live...on the planet. In the wry words of Richard Berryman, syndicated columnist with the *Hamilton Spectator*, "A bad day in Canada is better than a good day in any other country on the globe." An exaggeration, perhaps, but there's a grain of truth in it, as the United Nations (UN) might agree.

In 1994, the UN ranked 173 countries according to their quality of life, and Canada came first. It was the second time Canada had earned this distinction: the first was in 1992. The United Nations bases its ranking on standard of living, education, and life expectancy.

So, like parrots, turtles and redwood trees, Canadians can look forward to a long life – longer than can the citizens of all but seven countries in the world. According to UN figures, the average Canadian can expect to live 77.2 years, almost three years more than the average for industrial countries, and fourteen years more than the average for developing countries.

But the average Canadian will be outlived by the average Japanese. In Japan, life expectancy is 78.6 years, the longest anywhere in the world. At the other end of the scale is Sierra Leone, in West Africa, where the average Sierra Leonean can expect to live just 42.4 years.

Compared to the world at large, we are a highly educated society. Typically, we spend about 12.2 years in school. This puts us second only to the Americans, who average 12.4 years, and ahead of the Japanese at 10.8.

The United Nations estimates that out of a hundred Canadian adults, all but one can read, write and understand a short, simple sentence about their everyday life. This is as high a level of adult literacy as anywhere in the world.

Only five other countries have a higher standard of living than Canada, according to the UN's 1994 ranking; they are, in descending order: the United States, Switzerland, Luxembourg, Germany and Japan. On the other hand, we score higher than the Americans in life expectancy and higher than the Japanese in education, so overall the UN has ranked us the highest on its "human development index."

Compared to the other 23 member countries of the Organization for Economic Cooperation and Development (OECD), Canada spends a lot on education and health. For every dollar of our 1991 Gross Domestic Product (GDP), 7.4 cents went towards education. In Japan, the equivalent amount was a nickel, while in Norway it was 7.6 cents. In fact, the Norwegians led the OECD on this score, and we came second.

In terms of health, we spent $1 for every $10 of our 1991 Gross Domestic Product. We're second only to the Americans, who spent $1.34 for every $10 of GDP, and well ahead of the Japanese, who spent $0.66 for every $10 of their GDP.

TRADE BEATS Canada really does depend more heavily on trade than most of the G-7 countries. In 1994, the North American Free Trade Agreement, or NAFTA, came into effect. The same year we completed the Uruguay Round of the General Agreement on Tariffs and Trade (GATT). And, at the 1994 "Summit of the Americas," the so-called four amigos, Canada, the U.S., Mexico and Chile, began the process of bringing Chile into NAFTA.

Canada's trade in merchandise goods is hitting new heights. In 1994, exports came to $219 billion, the highest ever, and imports totalled $202 billion, also a record. Our biggest exports are machinery, equipment and automotive products. However, we also import large amounts of these goods.

On the other hand, we export forestry and energy products, but we import them in much smaller quantities. In 1993, these goods added a surplus of $33 billion to the merchandise trade total.

To the South Sir Winston Churchill described it as "an example to every country and a pattern for the future of the world." Canadian humorists have called it "five thousand miles of undefended boredom." Whatever the case, the 8,900 kilometre border Canada shares with the United States sees more trade in goods each year than any other in the world. In 1993, 80% of Canada's exports went to the U.S., which in turn supplied 73% of Canada's imports. Canada has a healthy

G-7: THE GROUP OF SEVEN The G-7 is the name given to the group of seven industrial nations with the largest economies. They are: Canada, France, Germany, Italy, Japan, the United Kingdom and the United States. In June 1995, Canada played host to the leaders of the G-7 countries at a summit meeting held in Halifax, Nova Scotia.

OECD: The Organization for Economic Cooperation and Development was formed in 1961. Its aim is to promote economic growth and development, employment, stability and world trade.

Today it numbers 24 members: Australia, Austria,* Belgium,* Canada, Denmark,* Finland,* France,* Germany,* Greece,* Iceland, Ireland,* Italy,* Japan, Luxembourg,* the Netherlands,* New Zealand, Norway, Portugal,* Spain,* Sweden,* Switzerland, Turkey, the United Kingdom* and the United States.

(* member of the European Union)

surplus in merchandise trade with the U.S. – nearly $20 billion in 1993, and easily surpassed this figure in 1994 with a surplus of $28.4 billion.

Across the Seas   Next to the United States, our biggest trading partners are Japan and the United Kingdom. We trade 4.5% of our merchandise exports and 4.9% of our merchandise imports with Japan, and 1.6% of our exports and 2.6% of our imports with the U.K. Over the last 10 years, these two countries have bought a smaller share of Canada's exports, while the United States has bought a larger share.

In imports, the trend is somewhat different: we have bought a larger proportion of our imports from Japan, while the proportion from the U.S. and U.K. has shrunk.

Whether it's coffee from Colombia or computers from South Korea, Canada is snapping up goods from developing countries. Imports from non-OECD countries (most of which are developing or newly industrialized countries) reached $19 billion in 1993, more than double the 1983 figure. Exports to other countries, however, have not kept up with this trend. Back in 1983, we exported to non-OECD countries $2.8 billion more than we imported, while in 1993 we actually imported $5.5 billion more than we exported.

TRADE IN SERVICES   Canada's international trade in services – travel, freight, business, government and other services – also set records in 1994, although here we came out on the short end: exports reached $30 billion, while imports hit $41 billion, for an overall deficit of $11 billion. Stronger exports of services resulted in a decrease of almost $3 billion in the trade in services deficit since 1993.

Income from investments flows out of Canada faster than it flows in: between October 1993 and October 1994, only $10 billion in investment income came into Canada from the outside, while $39 billion flowed out.

Foreign borrowing allows Canada to develop its economy by financing investments and other expenditures at home. But it also results in a steadily accumulating debt owed to other countries.

Canada's external liabilities – that is, the investments in Canada owned by foreigners – far outweigh our external assets (the investments we own in the rest of the world). In fact, Canada's net investment position – the difference between its external assets and liabilities – shows a widening gap. By the end of 1993, this "net external debt" had reached a record $313 billion, representing 12% of Canada's national wealth.

In fact, Canada consistently buys more than it sells in international markets, which has brought about this net external debt situation. In trading goods abroad, we make more money than we spend – $17.1 billion more in 1994. But that merchandise trade surplus is outweighed by a deficit

CANADA'S LARGEST COMPANIES
The top ten revenue earners of 1993:

		Revenues
1.	General Motors of Canada Ltd.*	$21,777,209,000
2.	Bell Canada Enterprises Inc.	$19,827,000,000
3.	Ford Motor Co. of Canada, Ltd.*	$15,918,400,000
4.	Chrysler Canada Ltd.*	$13,595,800,000
5.	George Weston Ltd.	$11,931,000,000
6.	Alcan Aluminium Ltd.	$9,329,280,000
7.	Ontario Hydro	$8,363,000,000
8.	Imasco Ltd.	$7,972,000,000
9.	Imperial Oil Ltd.*	$7,809,000,000
10.	The Thomson Corp.	$7,545,210,000

* Foreign-controlled

in non-merchandise trade, which includes services, investment income and transfers: in 1994, $41.9 billion more flowed out of Canada than into the country in non-goods trade, for an overall deficit of about $25 billion. By late 1994, an increased surplus in merchandise trade was helping keep the deficit lower than the previous year.

Nevertheless, our Current Account – the record of our overall international trade – has shown a deficit almost every year for the last four decades. This deficit has been balanced by a steady flow of investment into Canada from abroad.

GLOBAL TRENDS The big buzzword on the international trading scene these days is globalization. In a nutshell, it is this: a product which was once made and sold within the same country might today be designed in Canada using American funding, and assembled in South Korea using parts made in Japan. Then, with the help of a United Kingdom marketing firm, it might be sold all around the world.

In the 1960s, Canadian communications expert Marshall McLuhan heralded the onset of globalization when he coined the phrase "the global village." Technological changes such as the arrival of the computer, improved communications and new production techniques have all played a part in globalization, as have free trade and stronger economies among the developing nations, where wages are lower. It is a phenomenon that has had a significant impact on the Canadian economy over the last 10 to 15 years.

The Loonie on Foreign Shores More and more, the Canadian loonie, as we've dubbed our dollar, is "nesting" on foreign shores. Since the mid-1980s, our direct investment abroad has more than doubled to $115 billion by the end of 1993. Much of this has gone into the financial sector (especially banking), which absorbed one-quarter of all Canadian direct investment abroad in 1992.

When deciding where to invest, the loonie tends to fly south. By the end of 1993, 56% of what we invested abroad had gone to the United States. Interestingly, free trade agreements do not seem to have played a clear role in this; back in 1984, direct investment in the U.S. was considerably higher, at 69%.

Meanwhile, our investment in the European Union has increased: its share of Canada's total stock of direct investment abroad almost doubled from 11% in 1984 to 20% in 1993, and most of that investment was in the United Kingdom. By comparison, by the end of 1992, 9% of Canadian direct investment abroad was placed in Pacific Rim countries, including Australia and Japan.

Immigration has given a tremendous boost to Canada's external assets. In 1993, recent immigrants (mostly from Hong Kong and Taiwan) held a total of $29 billion in financial assets outside Canada, more than 10 times the 1983 figure.

CANADA'S LARGEST COMPANIES
The top ten employers of 1993:

		Employees
1.	Bell Canada Enterprises Inc.	118,000
2.	Imasco Ltd.	71,500
3.	McDonald's Restaurants of Canada Ltd.*	60,000
4.	Hudson's Bay Co.	56,500
5.	George Weston Ltd.	55,000
6.	Canada Post Corporation	52,000
7.	The Thomson Corp.	46,400
8.	Alcan Aluminium Ltd.	44,000
9.	Sears Canada Inc.*	41,075
10.	General Motors of Canada Ltd.*	40,572

* Foreign-controlled

Multinational Canada   Canadians are investing in ventures the world over but the corporations making those investments are fewer in number. In 1985, there were 1,555 Canadian enterprises holding a total of $54 billion in direct investment abroad; by 1991, there were only 1,396 companies with direct investment abroad, but the amount of that investment had almost doubled to $94 billion.

The rise of large multinational corporations has come hand-in-hand with globalization; as freer trade has reduced the tariffs that control the flow of goods and services between countries, multinationals have become more competitive, taking advantage of low production costs in developing countries and producing in large quantities for the global market.

Foreign Capital   As Canadians have increased their investments abroad, so have foreigners increased their investments in Canada – although not as quickly. In 1993, Canada's foreign direct investment had reached $146 billion, an increase of about 60% over 1985.

The United States accounts for the lion's share of foreign direct investment in Canada: 65% of the total. Over the last decade, the Americans' share has declined somewhat, while investments from the European Union and the Pacific Rim have gone up.

Maple Leaf in the Red?   Money also flows into Canada in the form of portfolio investments, such as stocks and bonds. These investments are one way for Canada to borrow money from abroad, and in recent years that borrowing has increased significantly. By the end of 1993, foreigners held $266 billion worth of Canadian bonds, more than double the 1985 figure.

"Buy!" "Sell!" "Buy!" "Sell!"   The familiar cry circles over a crowd of merchants and brokers vying for attention in the trading room. More and more, flows of capital are unregulated, responding to market forces alone, making the global money market a frenzied place.

One result is the spread of foreign ownership of Canadian bonds across an ever wider range of countries. Until the mid-1970s, the United States was the largest foreign holder of Canadian bonds, with around 80% of the total. By the end of 1993, this share had dropped to 42%, at which time Japan held 17%.

CANADA'S HIGH-TECH ECONOMY

The first intelligible words transmitted by telephone were, "Mr. Watson, come here, I want to see you," spoken by Alexander Graham Bell to his assistant. Invented in Canada in 1876, the telephone has set a Canadian standard for innovation in communications.

In 1972, Canada became the first country to launch a domestic geostationary satellite. Today, Canadian-pioneered

technologies such as digital switching and asynchronous transfer mode – a technique for sending digitized data through telephone wires thousands of times faster than usual – are powering the information highways being developed around the world.

ROOM TO MOVE   Picture this: by the time the last spike was driven home in 1885, the Canadian Pacific Railway stretched from Montreal to the Pacific Coast and measured more than 4,600 km. If you went the same distance south from Montreal instead of west, you would pass Caracas, the capital of Venezuela.

Geographically, we are the second largest country in the world, but Canadians make up only about one two-hundredth of the world's population. In the list of countries with the largest populations, Canada ranks thirty-third. China is first, the U.S. third, the Russian Federation sixth and Japan seventh.

In fact, if you were to divide Canada into the same number of portions as there are people, each Canadian would be standing in an area roughly the size of 27 baseball fields, or about 365,000 square metres of land. If you did this in the United States, each American would get about 3 baseball fields. In Japan, each Japanese would get just one-quarter of a baseball field. And in Hong Kong: less than a quarter of a baseball diamond.

Refuge   "I came to Canada as a refugee," writes journalist Joe Schlesinger, "and 45 years later, for me, Canada is a refuge still." Offering refuge is a long-standing Canadian tradition that continues to this day. In 1994, Canada took in some 20,000 people on humanitarian grounds. Most came from the former Yugoslavia followed by Sri Lanka, Iraq, Vietnam, Somalia and Iran.

Foreign Aid   It could be food for a pregnant mother in Cuba, a program to inoculate Pakistani children against polio, or improvements to an international airport in Jamaica. Canada has played a prominent role in helping other countries; in 1994-95, we offered the world some $2.6 billion in development aid.

In 1991, Canada was the seventh most generous supplier of aid in the world, behind the U.S., Japan, and the other G-7 countries. Comparing Canadian dollar contributions, our $110 per capita offering to official development aid was ahead of Japan's $99, and more than double that of the United States at $50.

Peacekeeping   Canadians have taken part in almost every peacekeeping mission undertaken by the UN. Canada has also been involved in several non-UN missions, including operations in Nigeria, Indochina, the Sinai, and the Balkans. Since 1947, one hundred Canadian personnel have lost their lives in peacekeeping operations.

In 1994, Canada had peacekeeping commitments in the former Yugoslavia, the Middle East, the Sinai (Egypt and Israel), Mozambique, Rwanda, the Golan Heights (Israel and Syria), Cambodia, the Iraq-Kuwait border, India and Pakistan, South Korea and Cyprus.

THE ENVIRONMENT "Canadians are the custodians of one of the largest parts of Planet Earth; it's vital that we see ourselves as the managers of this unique trust fund." As current chair of the Earth Council, Maurice Strong was referring to the pivotal role Canadians must play in preserving the global environment.

As guardians of one-fourteenth of the world's land, one-tenth of the world's forest and one-fifth of the world's wilderness, Canadians do have an enormous responsibility for the well-being of Planet Earth. In keeping with the World Conservation Union's objective of protecting 10% of the earth's surface as natural space, Canada has made a commitment to protect 12% of its land area from economic development.

At the 1992 United Nations Conference on Environment and Development (known as the Earth Summit) in Rio de Janeiro, Brazil, Canada moved quickly to sign the Convention on Biological Diversity, the Framework Convention on Climate Change, and Agenda 21, an international action plan to ensure that future development can be sustained without damage to the environment.

Canada's response to these agreements has included three initiatives: the Canadian Biodiversity Strategy, the National Action Program on Climate Change, and the *Projet de société*, a national partnership of government and indigenous, business and voluntary organizations that is working to translate the recommendations of Agenda 21 into action.

In 1992, the Canadian government banned the fishing of northern cod, Atlantic Canada's most important commercial fish stock, because of a severe depletion of the stock over the last decade or so.

In February 1994, the North Atlantic Fisheries Organization (of which Canada is a member) made the ban international, and in September 1994 it was broadened to include other endangered stocks, such as Greenland halibut (turbot).

In May 1994, the *Coastal Fisheries Protection Act* was amended, allowing Canada to use force if necessary to protect designated stocks from stateless and flag-of-convenience ships fishing on the Grand Banks outside the 200-mile zone. Just one week before the legislation came into force, seven such vessels were fishing in the area; by the time the legislation was in effect, they had all departed.

TRAVELLING THE GLOBE "I expect the greater part of my travels will be on paper," wrote Lucy Maud

Montgomery in 1899 — and then went on to write *Anne of Green Gables*. The inspirational setting of her novel, Green Gables House on Prince Edward Island, draws a third of a million tourists each year, including several thousand from Japan. Indeed, 13% of all Canada's overseas visitors are Japanese, second only to the United Kingdom with 18%. And the Japanese spend more — some $450 million in 1993 — than overseas visitors to Canada from any other country.

People are visiting Canada from overseas in increasing numbers: nearly 3.5 million in 1993, compared with less than a million in 1972. Americans make the most visits to Canada, averaging some 35 million per year over the last 20 years. And tourists are spending while they're here; in 1993 visitors spent almost $7 billion.

When Canadians travel abroad, their most popular destination, for obvious reasons, is the United States. But there are signs that we are increasingly adventuring further.

In 1981, Canadians made nearly 11 million overnight trips to the U.S., and about 1.5 million to other countries. Ten years later, we made some 19 million U.S. overnight trips (an increase of 76%), and 2.8 million to other countries (an increase of 91%). And in 1993, once memories of the Gulf War had receded and the recession had lifted, trips to the United States actually declined to 17.3 million, while overseas trips increased again to 3.3 million.

15 CENTURIES ON THE PHONE?! Canada has about 78 telephones for every 100 people. This puts us way ahead of the industrial world as a whole, which has 48 phones per 100 people, not to speak of the developing world, with just 3. Globally, the world has 13 phones for every 100 inhabitants. Only Switzerland, Denmark, Sweden, and the U.S. have more telephones per capita than Canada.

In 1993, the average Canadian spent half an hour on international phone calls. Canadians logged 807.8 million minutes on the phone to other countries — that's a total of about 15 centuries. Incoming calls from abroad amounted to 503.4 million minutes, close to a thousand years.

AND THE WINNER IS... if there were an Academy Award for best Statistical Agency, the Oscar would go to... Statistics Canada. That's the verdict of *The Economist*. In its "Good Statistics Guide," first published in 1991 and updated in 1993, the magazine rated the statistical agencies of several countries, including all of the G-7. It based its ranking on a poll of chief statisticians in those countries, institutions such as the International Monetary Fund, and users of international statistics. And both times, the winner was...Statistics Canada.

$\mathcal{P}$ H O T O G R A P H I C $\mathcal{C}$ R E D I T S

$\mathscr{B}$IBLIOGRAPHY

SELECTED SOURCES

Chapter 1

Statistics Canada:

Human Activity and the Environment (1994)	Cat. No. 11-509E
General Review of the Mineral Industry	Cat. No. 26-201
Canadian Agriculture at a Glance	Cat. No. 96-301

Canada. Environment Canada. *The State of the Environment.* Ottawa, 1991.

Rayburn, Alan. *Naming Canada.* Toronto: University of Toronto Press, 1994.

Chapter 2

Statistics Canada:

Language, Tradition, Health, Lifestyle, and Social Issues	Cat. No. 89-533
Religions in Canada	Cat. No. 93-319
Knowledge of Languages – The Nation	Cat. No. 93-318
Schooling, Work and Related Activities, Income and Expenses	Cat. No. 89-534
Age and Sex	Cat. No. 94-327

The Vanier Institute of the Family, *Profiling Canada's Families*, Ottawa, 1994.

Canada. Canadian Advisory Council On the Status of Women. *110 Canadian Statistics on Work and the Family*. Ottawa, 1994.

Canada. Citizenship and Immigration Canada. *A Broader Vision: Immigration and Citizenship Plan 1995 to the Year 2000 – Annual Report to Parliament*. Ottawa, 1994.

Chapter 3

Statistics Canada:

Education in Canada 1992-1993	Cat. No. 81-229
Health Reports	Cat. No. 82-003
Juristat	Cat. No. 85-002
Education Quarterly Review	Cat. No. 81-003
Causes of Death	Cat. No. 84-208

Health and Welfare Canada. *Canada's Health Promotion Survey 1990 – Technical Report*. Ottawa, 1993.

Chapter 4

Statistics Canada:

Book Publishing	Cat. No. 87-210

SELECTED SOURCES

Film and Video — Cat. No. 87-204
Heritage Institutions — Cat. No. 87-207
Performing Arts — Cat. No. 87-209
Radio and Television Broadcasting — Cat. No. 56-204
Television Viewing — Cat. No. 87-208
Periodical Publishing — Cat. No. 87-203
Focus on Culture — Cat. No. 87-004

Mckellar, Iain. "Cultural Participation in Canada." Unpublished paper, Statistics Canada, 1994.

Corbeil, Jean-Pierre. "Sport Participation in Canada." Unpublished paper. Statistics Canada, 1994.

Chapter 5
Statistics Canada:

Labour Force Annual Averages 1989-1994 — Cat. No. 71-529
Historical Labour Force Statistics 1994 — Cat. No. 71-201
Retail Trade — Cat. No. 63-005
Income Distributions by Size in Canada — Cat. No. 13-207
Family Incomes — Cat. No. 13-208
The Consumer Price Index — Cat. No. 62-001

Statistics Canada. *CANSIM* (CANSIM, Statistics Canada's public electronic database, is a comprehensive source of Canadian economic data. Information on gaining access is available at Statistics Canada's Regional Reference Centres, listed in the back pages of this book).

Cross, Philip. Unpublished paper on Canada's current economic conditions. Statistics Canada, 1994.

Chapter 6
Statistics Canada:

Canada's Balance of International Payments — Cat. No. 67-001
Canada's International Investment Position — Cat. No. 67-202
International Travel, Travel Between Canada and Other Countries — Cat. No. 66-201
Canada's International Transactions in Services, 1992-1993 — Cat. No. 67-203
Travel-log — Cat. No. 87-003
Canada's Balance of International Payments, Historical Statistics 1926 to 1992 — Cat. No. 67-508

United Nations Development Program. Human Development Report 1994. United Nations Development Program and

SELECTED SOURCES

Oxford University Press. New York and Oxford, 1994.

Organization for Economic Development and Cooperation. *The OECD in Figures 1994 Edition*. Paris, 1994.

_____.*OECD Economic Outlook. Nos. 53-56*, Paris, 1993, 1994.

_____.*OECD Economic Outlook*. Paris, 1994.

Canada. Citizenship and Immigration Canada.*Immigration Statistics 1992*. Ottawa, 1994.

Canada. Canadian International Development Agency. *Annual Report 1992-1993*. Ottawa, 1994.

Common Sources

Statistics Canada:

The Canada Year Book, 1994	Cat. No. 11-402E
Canada: A Portrait, 54th Edition	Cat. No. 11-403E
Canadian Social Trends	Cat. No. 11-008E
Family and Friends	Cat. No. 11-612E
Perspectives on Labour and Income	Cat. No. 75-001E
Canadian Economic Observer	Cat. No. 11-010
Report on the Demographic Situation in Canada	Cat. No. 91-209E

The Daily	Cat. No. 11-001E

Prentice Hall, Statistics Canada. *Focus on Canada Series*. Ottawa, 1994.

Colombo, John Robert, ed. *Colombo's New Canadian Quotations*. Edmonton: Hurtig, 1987.

Colombo, John Robert, ed. *The Dictionary of Canadian Quotations*. Toronto: Stoddart, 1991.

Other Sources
Publications, interviews, and/or unpublished material:

Canadian Heritage, Parks Canada, Citizenship Promotion
Canadian Human Rights Commission
Department of Citizenship and Immigration
Department of Fisheries and Oceans
Department of Foreign Affairs and International Trade
Department of Finance
Department of National Defence
Embassy of the United States
Environment Canada
Health Canada
Justice Canada
The Bank of Canada

STATISTICS CANADA

REGIONAL REFERENCE CENTRES

Telecommunications Device for the Hearing Impaired
1-800-363-7629.

Toll Free Order Only Line (Canada and the United States)
1-800-267-6677.

If outside the local calling area, please dial the toll free number for your region.

Atlantic Region

Serving the provinces of Newfoundland and Labrador, Nova Scotia, Prince Edward Island and New Brunswick.

Statistics Canada, Advisory Services
1170 Market Street
Halifax, Nova Scotia
B3J 3M3

Toll free:	1-800-565-7192
Local calls:	(902) 426-5331
Fax:	(902) 426-9538

Quebec Region

Statistics Canada, Advisory Services
200 René Levesque Boulevard West
East Tower, 4th Floor

Montreal, Quebec
H2Z 1X4

Toll free:	1-800-361-2831
Local calls:	(514) 283-5725
Fax:	(514) 283-9350

National Capital Region

Statistics Canada, Statistical Reference Centre
R.H. Coats Building Lobby
Tunney's Pasture
Ottawa, Ontario
K1A 0T6

Local calls:	(613) 951-8116
Fax:	(613) 951-0581

Ontario Region

Statistics Canada, Advisory Services
25 St. Clair Avenue East, 10th Floor
Toronto, Ontario
M4T 1M4

Toll free:	1-800-263-1136
Local calls:	(416) 973-6586
Fax:	(416) 973-7475

Prairie Region

Serving the provinces of Manitoba, Saskatchewan, Alberta and the Nothwest Territories.

Statistics Canada, Advisory Services
344 Edmonton Street, Suite 300
Winnipeg, Manitoba
R3B 3L9

Toll free: 1-800-661-7828
Local calls: (204) 983-4020
Fax: (204) 983-7543

Statistics Canada
Advisory Services
2002 Victoria Avenue, 9th Floor
Regina, Saskatchewan
S4P 0R7

Toll free: 1-800-667-7164
Local calls: (306) 780-5405
Fax: (306) 780-5403

Statistics Canada, Advisory Services
10001 Bellamy Hill, 9th Floor
Edmonton, Alberta
T5J 3B6

Toll free: 1-800-563-7828
Local calls: (403) 495-3027
Fax: (403) 495-5318

Statistics Canada, Advisory Services
138 Fourth Avenue South East, Room 401
Calgary, Alberta
T2G 4Z6

Toll free: 1-800-882-5616
Local calls: (403) 292-6717
Fax: (403) 292-4958

Pacific Region

Serving the province of British Columbia and the Yukon Territory.

Statistics Canada, Advisory Services
757 West Hastings Street, Suite 300
Vancouver, British Columbia
V6C 3C9

Toll free: 1-800-663-1551
Local calls: (604) 666-3691
Fax: (604) 666-4863

Index

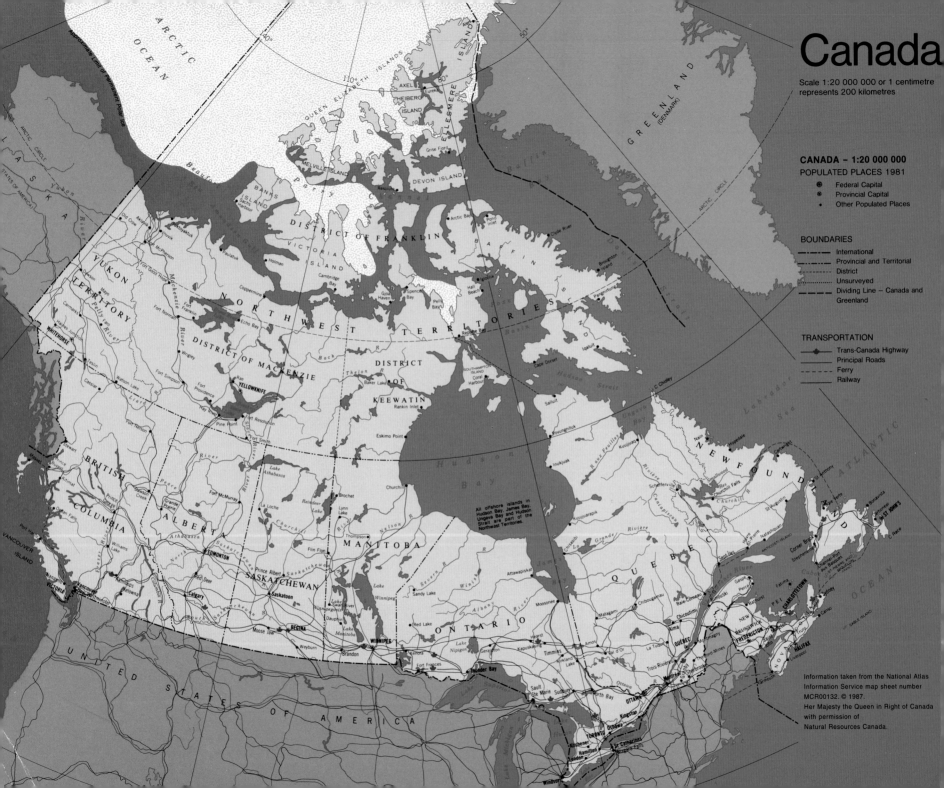

Canada

Scale 1:20 000 000 or 1 centimetre
represents 200 kilometres

CANADA – 1:20 000 000

POPULATED PLACES 1981

- ⊛ Federal Capital
- ⊚ Provincial Capital
- • Other Populated Places

BOUNDARIES

—·—·—	International
————	Provincial and Territorial
- - - - -	District
··········	Unsurveyed
— — —	Dividing Line – Canada and Greenland

TRANSPORTATION

◆———	Trans-Canada Highway
———	Principal Roads
– – – –	Ferry
———	Railway

All offshore islands in
Hudson Bay, James Bay,
Ungava Bay and Hudson
Strait are part of the
Northwest Territories.

Information taken from the National Atlas
Information Service map sheet number
MCR00132. © 1987.
Her Majesty the Queen in Right of Canada
with permission of
Natural Resources Canada.